# TOPKAPI PALACE
## Inside and Out

A Guide to The Topkapi Palace Museum and Grounds

## Claire Karaz

Photographs: Murat Oğurlu

# TOPKAPI PALACE
## Inside and Out
A Guide to The Topkapi Palace Museum and Grounds

### Claire Karaz
Photographs: Murat Oğurlu

ISBN: 975-6663-49-9

First edition: 2004
Photographs: Murat Oğurlu
Layout&Design: Murat Oğurlu
Cover design: Deniz Akkol
Color separation: NEF Grafik
Printing and binding: Berdan Matbaası

Published by:
Çitlembik Publications
Şeyh Bender Sokak 18/5
Asmalımescit Tünel
80050 Istanbul TURKEY
www.citlembik.com.tr

&

Nettleberry, LLC.
44030 123rd St.
Eden, South Dakota 57232
www.nettleberry.com

# Contents

This book is the fruit of my profession as a guide and my own search for answers to questions others have asked me –not to mention the ones I've asked myself– every time I've guided a group around Topkapi Palace. Hence the structure of the book, designed to be a step-by-step tour guide accompanied by fascinating historical tidbits as well as thought-provoking questions (and possible answers).

Special thanks and acknowledgements are due to several individuals who helped make this book a reality. I've had the great fortune of meeting Caroline Finkel, who has given me numerous books to read, including her own manuscript, from which I have greatly benefitted in the course of composing this guidebook. Other works that I have especially relied upon and which therefore deserve special mention here are Gülrü Necipoğlu's book on Topkapi, Leslie Peirce's book on the imperial Harem, and Halil Inalcık's, *The Ottoman Empire: The Classical Age 1300-1600*. Further details about these and other sources can be found in the short bibliography at the end of the book. Many thanks to Filiz Çağman, Topkapi Museum Director, for her invaluable assistance, Murat Oğurlu for his beautiful photographs and the patience he showed as we matched the appropriate images with the corresponding text, and my friend Elif Pekin for knowing exactly what visual effect I had in mind. I especially thank Nancy Öztürk for taking on this project and Amy Spangler for reading and correcting it. Without my husband, Süleyman, this would never have come about.

Topkapi Palace, as viewed from the Sea of Marmara

# Useful Information

- Telephone number: +90 (212) 512-0480
- Open every day from 9:00 a.m. to 4:00 p.m., except Tuesday's (Winter)
- Open every day from 9:00 a.m. to 6:00 p.m., except Tuesday's (Summer)

- **Topkapi Palace** and **Treasury** entrance tickets are available in the first courtyard, in front of the Middle Gate, on the right:
    - Topkapi Palace Museum              13 million TL/8 euro
    - Treasury section                   13 million TL/8 euro

- **Harem** section tickets are available in the second courtyard on the left in front of the Harem entrance:
    - Harem section                      13 million TL/8 euro

- IMPORTANT! Please note that general admission does not include entrance to the Harem or Treasury sections; entrance tickets to those sections must be purchased separately.
- Summer hours may be extended and may be open on Tuesday's; call ahead to find out.
- Bank/change office is located next to the ticket office in front of the Middle Gate on the right.
- W.C. is also located next to the ticket office in front of the Middle Gate on the right and in the Mecidiye Pavilion (Konyalı Restaurant) in the Terraced Gardens.
- A small café is located to the right of the Harem entrance in the second courtyard, while Konyalı Restaurant and Cafeteria are in the Terraced Gardens.
- Public transportation: Sultan Ahmet Tramway stop on Divan Yolu is a short walk to the Imperial Gate.
- Taxis are easily found in front of the Imperial Gate and at the Gülhane Park entrance near the Processions Pavilion.
- If your time is limited, it is advised that you head straight to the museum entrance and begin your tour with the second courtyard.

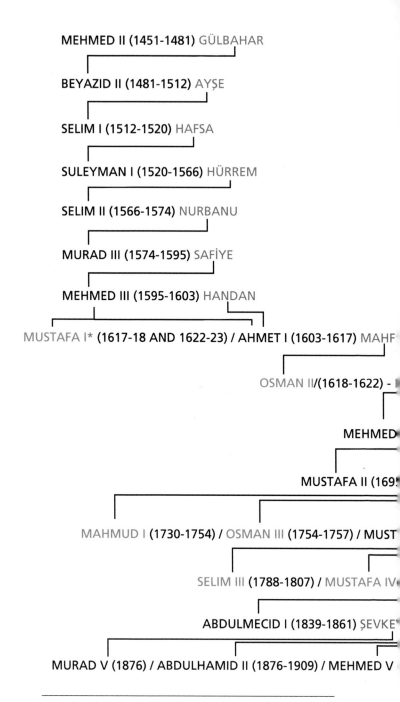

**MEHMED II (1451-1481)** GÜLBAHAR

**BEYAZID II (1481-1512)** AYŞE

**SELIM I (1512-1520)** HAFSA

**SULEYMAN I (1520-1566)** HÜRREM

**SELIM II (1566-1574)** NURBANU

**MURAD III (1574-1595)** SAFİYE

**MEHMED III (1595-1603)** HANDAN

MUSTAFA I* (1617-18 AND 1622-23) / **AHMET I (1603-1617)** MAHF

OSMAN II/(1618-1622) -

**MEHMED**

**MUSTAFA II (169**

MAHMUD I (1730-1754) / OSMAN III (1754-1757) / **MUST**

**SELIM III (1788-1807)** / MUSTAFA IV

**ABDULMECID I (1839-1861)** ŞEVKE

MURAD V (1876) / ABDULHAMID II (1876-1909) / **MEHMED V**

Names in red are the women who produced future sultans.
Names in green are sultans who did not produce heirs.
Years refer to the reign, not the life-span, of the sultan.
\* Indicates that the name of the mother is unknown.
\*\* Last heir to the throne, served as caliph only.

# OTTOMAN SULTANS FROM

## 1453 to 1923

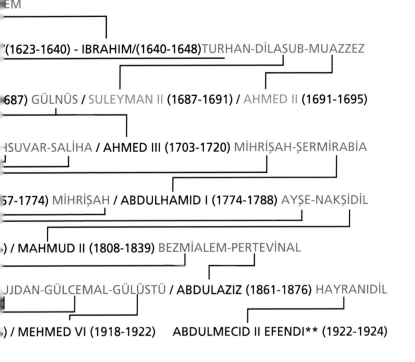

EM

(1623-1640) - IBRAHIM/(1640-1648)TURHAN-DİLAŞUB-MUAZZEZ

687) GÜLNÜS / SULEYMAN II (1687-1691) / AHMED II (1691-1695)

HSUVAR-SALİHA / AHMED III (1703-1720) MİHRİŞAH-ŞERMİRABİA

57-1774) MİHRİŞAH / ABDULHAMID I (1774-1788) AYŞE-NAKŞİDİL

) / MAHMUD II (1808-1839) BEZMİALEM-PERTEVİNAL

JJDAN-GÜLCEMAL-GÜLÜSTÜ / ABDULAZIZ (1861-1876) HAYRANIDİL

) / MEHMED VI (1918-1922)    ABDULMECID II EFENDI** (1922-1924)

# Introduction

When the Ottoman Sultan Mehmed II took Constantinople in 1453, he immediately moved the capital of his rapidly growing empire to his newest conquest: Constantinople, now Istanbul. It was, without a doubt, the most important city of the Mediterranean world and the key to Ottoman sovereignty over the Balkans and Eastern Mediterranean region. Just a year later, construction of a palace for the sultan commenced in the city center. With its gardens surrounded by high walls, it occupied a large area that included the present grounds of Istanbul University. Soon realizing that he needed a more secluded area for his resi-

Topkapi Palace, as viewed from the Golden Horn

dence and administrative center, however, Mehmed "the Conqueror" began working in 1459 on his "New Palace," later to be known as Topkapi. He first had the land of the promontory, today's Saray Burnu, cleared and terraced in preparation for the construction of the new palace, which would ultimately be completed in 1478. The promontory was specifically chosen as a place that would provide seclusion and perhaps safety from rebellion and plague as well as a symbolic location looking over the seas from Europe to Asia.

The grounds of the palace are on a triangular promontory that juts out into the Sea of Marmara to the southeast and the Golden Horn to the northwest, with its tip facing north to the opening of the Bosphorus Straits. The ancient acropolis of Byzantium was located on this site as well and until the thirteenth century many churches and palaces stood here. However, by the time of the conquest, these buildings were in ruin and mostly underground, as the city had shifted west leaving the Palace Point, then known as the Olive Grove, abandoned. As was common practice, the spoglia, or remains of the buildings, that had once occupied the acropolis provided building material for the construction of the "New Palace."

Just as it was at the time of the construction, the palace's main entrance today is located on the land side, just in back of Haghia Sophia. It is a short walk to the hippodrome and the main city road known as the Council's Road (Divan Yolu), which has led from the land walls to the center for centuries. One of Mehmed's first acts after taking Constantinople was to convert the Great Church of Haghia Sophia into a mosque. Thus, his palace was just behind the great mosque of the newly founded capital of the Ottoman empire. He brought artists and artisans from Persia and Italy as well as employing many from his own empire to build his palace, yet the layout essentially reflects an Ottoman encampment ready for siege with private inner quarters buffered by outer administrative and service areas. It is Mehmed's personality that is the ultimate key to the project.

Portrait of Sultan Mehmed II

The palace has been called "Topkapı Sarayı" since the nineteenth century. The name literally means "The Cannon Gate Palace." At the time of its construction in the fifteenth century, the palace was known as the "New Palace." Later it would be dubbed the "Imperial Palace," a name it would carry until the nineteenth century. The name "Topkapi" originally comes from a very large wooden pavilion called Topkapi Palace because of its proximity to a sea gate located near the tip of the promontory. Built by Sultan Mahmud I in the eighteenth century, this building burned in 1862 leaving nothing behind – except for its name, which it passed on to the larger palace complex. The name Topkapi came to imply the Imperial Palace when the Dolmabahçe Palace, completed in 1856, became the Ottoman Sultans' new residence. The second half of its name, "Saray," is a word of Persian origin meaning "palace," which was misinterpreted as "serraglio" in Italian meaning "closed" or "locked," a connotation that would be passed on to other European languages as well. After the construction of the "New Palace," Mehmed's first palace came to be known as the "Old Palace" and it continued to be used as a residence for the retired ladies of the Harem. The "New Palace" or "Topkapi Palace" was the Ottoman Sultans' royal residence and administrative center

for nearly four hundred years until 1856, when these were transferred to Dolmabahçe Palace. Although Topkapi Palace has undergone a variety of changes and additions over the centuries, the plan remains essentially that of Mehmed II.

Portrait of Sultan Mehmed II-copy

## QUESTIONS
1. Why is Sultan Mehmed II called "the Conqueror"?
2. What is the significance of Topkapi Palace's location?
3. There are two different portraits of Mehmed II shown on this and the preceding page; can you guess which one is by the Italian and which one is by the Persian artist? Why?

# Imperial Gate and Outer Walls

The main entrance gate to the palace is the Bab-ı Hümayün, Arabic for "**The Imperial Gate**." In the arch just above the gateway, you can see three kinds of calligraphic Arabic script, one above the other. The lowest one is a sultan's monogram ("tuğra"). In this case, it is that of Mahmud II to commemorate some remodeling he had commissioned in the nineteenth century. His monogram appears in many places since he was the last sultan to reside continuously in Topkapi. Mahmud was also an expert calligrapher, and some of the monograms are attributed to his own hand.

Just above it, in a long rectangular frame, is the foundation inscription of Mehmed II. It reads: "By the grace of God, and by His approval, the foundations of this auspicious castle were laid, and its parts were solidly joined together to strengthen peace and tranquility, by the hand of the Sultan of the two Continents, and the Emperor of the two Seas, the Shadow of God in this world and the next, the Favorite of God on the two

Horizons, the Monarch of the Terraqueous Orb, the Conqueror of the Castle of Constantinople, the Father of Conquest Sultan Mehmed Khan, son of Sultan

The Imperial Gate after recent cleaning

Murad Khan son of Sultan Mehmed Khan, may God make eternal his empire, and exalt his residence above the most lucid stars of the firmament, in the blessed month of Ramadan of the year 883." (Nov-Dec 1478)

In the curve of the arch in elaborate calligraphic script called "thuluth," there is an inscription from the Koran. It reads: "Truly the God-fearing will be amidst gardens and water springs. Enter therein in peace and security. And we shall strip away all rancor from their breasts, so they will be like brothers sitting on thrones face to face. No fatigue shall ever spite

Tuğra of Mahmud II

them, neither shall they ever be driven from here." (The Holy Koran, Surah 15 Al-Hijr; 45-48)

The Imperial Gate

even though the sultans no longer lived in the palace by then.

Most of the towers in the walls are square while two are octagonal and one is dodecagonal. If you do not enter the Imperial Gate, but rather walk down Soğuk Çeşme Street to the left, as you face the gate, try to count the square towers behind the wooden houses until you get to the dodecagonal one.

In the miniature of the Imperial Gate, you can see a second storey. This had several functions that changed over time. For example, it served as a dormitory for gate keepers and on occasion the sultan would make appearances to his people from the middle window of the upper floor in honor of one of the religious festivals or before going on a campaign. In keeping with Mehmed's withdrawal from the public, however, the practice of the sultan appearing here stopped shortly after its construction. The second storey was finally destroyed by fire in the nineteenth century. After the fire, Sultan Abdulaziz ordered the marble facing on the Imperial Gate

Processions' Pavilion

Wall section map

Located just to the side of today's Gülhane Park entrance, a lovely onion-shaped dome crowns this tower that was built as a pavilion. It was known as the **Processions' Pavilion** (Alay Köşkü) because from his room in its tower the sultan used to watch processions of the guilds showing their finest goods. It was from the windows of this tower that the sultan also gave ear to the complaints of rebels during periods of social unrest and that the corpses of traitors were thrown for the crowds to see that justice had been given.

The Sublime Porte

of the empire moved from the second courtyard of Topkapi Palace to this new location in the eighteenth century when it outgrew its original location within the second courtyard. For this reason, the Sublime Porte was the expression used to refer to the Ottoman gov-

Across the street from the Processions' Pavillion is the fancy rococo entrance gate, Bab-ı Ali, once known as the "Sublime Porte." The "Divan" council meetings of the viziers concerning administrative and judicial matters

ernment. The street that divides the Palace from this gate is the "Alemdar" or "Flag Bearers'" Street. Today the Sublime Porte leads to the Governor's offices.

## QUESTIONS

4. What do we learn about Mehmed II from the inscriptions he had carved on the entrance to his palace? How did he view himself and his dynasty?
5. What shapes are the two towers in the wall to the right of the Imperial Gate?
6. Does the Imperial Gate look more like a palace entrance or a fortress? Why? How does the miniature on page 16 differ from the gate you see today?
7. In 1810, Sultan Mahmud II had the dodecagonal tower known as the "Processions' Pavilion" shortened. What purpose might this have served?

# First Courtyard

The weaponry once hanging from the walls of the vestibule of the Imperial Gate was to remind visitors to leave their weapons behind and also to reinforce the fact that the palace was a peaceful haven. Entering armed was absolutely forbidden.

Today, the first courtyard resembles a park, its paths lined with plane trees planted in the twentieth century. Open to the public, any unarmed person was free to pass through the Imperial Gate and enter this courtyard. The area was conceived as a huge open space for ceremonies and processions involving hundreds or even thousands of people. For example, twenty-five thousand janissaries, members of the sultan's elite military unit, attended Mehmed II's funeral here. Today, a janissary band, or "Mehtar," marches through the first courtyard on Wednesday afternoons between 3:00 and 4:00 P.M., resplendent with traditional instruments and uniforms.

Service buildings once stood on either side of the courtyard. For example, an infirmary and bathhouse for royal pages once stood immediately to the right, just inside the entrance, far from the inner core of the palace to keep disease at bay. A eunuch was in charge of it as well as the wood storehouses nearby. The infirmary patients were treated with music and herbal medicines. It is known that sometimes the royal pages feigned illness to be able to meet relatives and

Hospital for pages

drink wine here, since the first courtyard was open to the public. Further to the right, there was a royal bakery where both refined white and coarse dark breads were made. Very little remains of these buildings because most of them were made of rubble and therefore easily collapsed over time.

The Turkish military controls a part of the first courtyard down to the Sea of Marmara; this area is easily distinguishable

The First Courtyard / Janissary band (above)

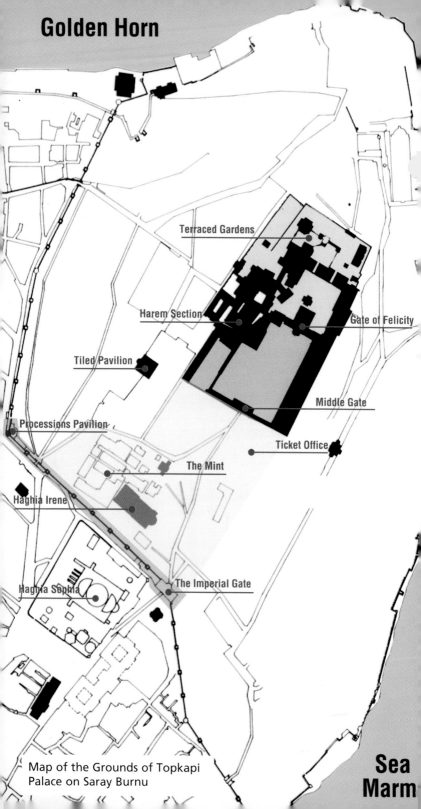

Golden Horn

Terraced Gardens

Harem Section

Gate of Felicity

Tiled Pavilion

Middle Gate

Processions Pavilion

Ticket Office

The Mint

Haghia Irene

Haghia Sophia

The Imperial Gate

Map of the Grounds of Topkapi
Palace on Saray Burnu

Sea
Marm

as it is marked off by barbed wire fencing.

Nowadays a building for guards stands to the left of the entrance where a dormitory for about 120 novice pages once stood. Before the boys could enter the inner palace as royal pages, they ran errands for the royal pages and carried wood. The storehouse for wood and a stable for the wood-carrying oxen used to provide firewood for the palace once occupied the space behind the dormitory. This wood came from the forests around the Black Sea and the young men from the palace who needed to build up their muscles carried the wood from the ships anchored below.

Haghia Irene

The most prominent structure in the first courtyard, which predates the palace by about 900 years, is **Haghia Irene**, Church of Divine Peace. This sixth century church functioned as an armory for the palace. There has been a lot of speculation about why Mehmed did not convert the church into a mosque. It is known that he collected Christian relics and was fond enough of his Christian step-mother, a Serbian princess, to give her a relic of Saint John the Baptist. An armory was needed and the building provided ample space within sturdy walls for it. When the craze for archaeology finally hit the Ottomans in the nineteenth century, precious antiquities were stored in Haghia Irene until the Archaeological Museums were built for their display. Haghia Irene also provided a great deal of building material for the palace and other buildings in Istanbul, so much so that a sixteenth century source said it might topple if even one more single column were to be removed.

Just behind Haghia Irene lie

The First Courtyard

Haghia Irene / Armory

family almost continuously until 1880. The Mint and Haghia Irene are used today for special exhibits or summer concerts. Every two years (odd numbered) Istanbul hosts a Biennale featuring contemporary

The Mint

artists' works exhibited in these buildings as well as others around the city.

Turning left past the Mint into Osman Hamdi Bey Street, a slope leads to the Gülhane Park, which was originally part of the outer gardens of the Topkapi Palace. The entrance to the Istanbul Archaeological Museums is on the right as you walk down Osman Hamdi Bey Street. Should you buy a ticket to visit the museums, you will see several buildings that house its collections; the building to the far left is the **Tiled Pavilion** (Çinili Köşkü). While today it houses a lovely collection of Turkish ceramics, the building itself is of particular historical and architectural significance. It was originally constructed by Mehmed II in 1472 to commemorate his conquest of the

the walls of the **Mint**, which extend to a small road leading down to the left. The remains of the Mint you see today are those of an eighteenth century group of buildings partially in ruin, though excavations have shown that a mint was located here even in the fifteenth century. Superintendent of the Imperial Mint was an important, highly coveted position. Held by Jews during much of the seventeenth and early eighteenth centuries, after 1757 the position was occupied by members of the Armenian Catholic Duzian

Gold coin

Haghia Irene-Armory

The Mint

Karaman region in central Anatolia, a region heavily influenced by Timurid Persian tastes. It has been suggested that it was conceived as part of a trio of pavilions in the outer grounds, each in an architectural style representing a part of the realm of Mehmed II: Persian, Greek, and Ottoman.

The Tiled Pavilion is a splendid example of Mehmed II's interest in the Timurid style architecture of Persia and is the only pavilion of this type in the entire world to have survived up to the present day. Most likely, architects came from the Karaman region to build it, although Persian ceramicists might have been brought in to produce the fantastic tiles. The structure is made of brick and stone with a lead domed roof. Originally, the porch colonnade was made of wood, but it burned in the eighteenth century and was rebuilt with the present marble columns by the order of Sultan Abdulhamit I.

The façade is also a showcase for different styles of calligraphic script in Arabic as well as Persian. Both languages use the same Arabic lettering, as did Ottoman Turkish until the foundation of the Turkish Republic. Written in Persian using the thuluth style script, the foundation inscription is in two intertwined levels above the doorway. The inscription extols the beauty of the pavilion, comparing it to paradise: "The emerald dome is like the starry dome of heaven built on the mansion of paradise reaching the constellations… The delicate air inside will make even the dried bones of the dead come back to life…" The iwan arched entrance is decorated in a style known as mirrored script with giant geometric "kufic" lettering on the arched section while small tiles, like tesserae, form the words "Allah" and "Mohammed" in square kufic script on the exteri-

*Archaeological Museums Entrance*

*The Tiled Pavilion*

Tiled iwan entrance

or walls. The magnificent turquiose blues and violet colors of the tiles are produced by using cobalt, which at the time was

Tiled Pavilion interior

found exclusively in the mountains of Iran near Kashan.

The Tiled Pavilion was a pleasure palace. From its east side pages could be watched as they played jereed on the then sandy playing ground, while the west side overlooked an artificial lake. A popular sport during the Ottoman period, Jereed was played on horseback between two teams, the members of which would stay about 100 meters apart at either end of the field and throw blunt wooden spears at one another as they tried to unseat the opponent team members from their mounts. Points were taken off if a horse was hit. It is still played, especially in eastern Turkey, although by slightly different rules. Used as a residence for eunuchs of the palace sometime during the late seventeenth century, the pavilion was abandoned after the fire of 1737 and remained in a state of disuse until renovations were carried out in the 1780's.

The pavilion has two floors: a high basement floor and a first floor. The interior is perfectly symmetrical with the side rooms connected by small passages to the central rooms. While the corner rooms of the building, being warmed by fireplaces, were used as winter retreats, the basement floor would have served as a cool summer space. Although the Tiled Pavilion has been renovated several times, it remains an outstanding example of Timurid architecture.

Now return to the first courtyard central path leading to the Middle Gate. To the left behind a low curtain wall, there used to be workshops for straw-mat makers, carpenters, stonecutters and blacksmiths, tailors, painters (miniaturists), calligraphers, carpet weavers, and many more guilds, known mostly from miniature paintings since only traces of these

structures survive. There were between forty and fifty different guilds, mostly located within the palace grounds, though a few were located near the hippodrome. The number of artists and artisans employed by the palace varied over the years: three hundred and sixty in 1500, six hundred and thirty-six in 1566, nine hundred in 1600,

Portrait of Sultan Selim

and down to one hundred and eighty-six in 1790. Some of the miniatures in the manuscript collection of Topkapi palace were painted in these workshops, just as some of the sultans' kaftans and

*wling Demons* by Mehmet Siyah Kalem

archer rings were created here. Though they rarely signed their work, we learn the names and often the origin of these artists from the records kept of their wages. Thus we know that Turks, Persians, Hungarians, Albanians, and others worked together to produce the many splendid objects that came out of these workshops.

One of the world's richest collections of Islamic miniature paintings and calligraphy belongs to Topkapi Museum. It used to be housed in one of the halls that separate the third courtyard from the Terraced Gardens. While the museum is trying to find suitable conditions for their display, as of yet it remains uncertain where or when this will take place. Some of the works came to the palace as

booty after conquests, while others were gifts to promote peace. Many of them were commissioned by the sultan and made in the workshops of the first courtyard.

One famous group attributed to the artist Mehmed Siyah Kalem ("Black Pen Mehmet") may have come as booty from the Timurid capital of Herat, now in Afghanistan, though the artist has been assumed to be of Uighur or Mongol origin, which are peoples of the Asian steppe. The unusual monstrous demons playfully inhabiting the paintings are thought to be related to shamanistic rituals of that region. Since there is no text with which to associate this group of paintings, art historians do not all agree on the origin and meaning of these works of art.

Another highlight of the collection is a fascinating series of miniatures by Matrakçi Nasuh.

*Kerbela, Iraq* by Matrakçi Nasuh

Commissioned by Suleyman the Magnificent, they consist of maps of cities as far away as Nice on the Mediterranean to Erzurum in eastern Turkey. They once served strategic military purposes and are today a valuable source to urban historians.

The colorful illustrations to the various Surname-i Hümayun, or Books of Festivals, let us peek into the lives of the sultans. In one such book dating to the time of Sultan Ahmet III in the early eighteenth century, we see a procession of the palace guilds and the circumcision ceremony of the sultan's young sons. In addition to their intrinsic aesthetic value, these comic strip-like miniatures are a source for understanding buildings that are no longer standing, designs in textiles that no longer exist, or rituals that are no longer practiced.

The Executioner's Fountain

As you approach the Middle Gate, to the right before reaching the bank and shop, you see a fountain in the wall where the executioners washed their hands and swords after decapitating important enemies of the empire. It is apparently an old tradition only that gives **The Executioner's Fountain** its name, since the inscription tells us that the present fountain was built by Abdulhamid II at a time when the corps of executioners had already been banned, their last days on the job having coincided with the dissolution of the Janissaries in 1826. Most likely, this fountain replaced an earlier one that really did serve the purpose ascribed to it by its name.

The executioners were a military unit made up mostly of converted Croatians and Copts whose job it was to execute. Executions were usually carried out by some combination of strangulation and beheading, often in public places. There was a small prison within the Middle

Marble posts

Gate for those who committed the heinous crime of treason against the state. The heads of these criminals were stuffed with cotton or straw and displayed on marble posts in the first courtyard for the public to see, after having been executed in the second courtyard under the gaze of the sultan. The heads of many viziers, governors, deputies, and officials of the state decorated marble posts in the first courtyard, the Imperial Gate entrance, and the Processions' Pavilion. Of 178 grand viziers, thirty-two met violent deaths.

Again on the right, behind the ticket office, there was once a water works with water-wheels connected to an aqueduct. This device served to collect water in cisterns used to provide the palace with constantly running water. A halberdier used to control the flow so that wherever the sultan happened to be, the nearby fountains sprung with water. An ancient well located and restored in the sixteenth century by the architect Sinan became the center of the water works for the gardens. Archaeological research has shown that it dates to the first century B.C.E.

To the the left of the Middle Gate once stood a small octagonal pavilion where visitors could present their petitions to officials of the court to be heard by the members

of the council. It was also at this pavilion that the sultan occasionally appeared before his troops before campaigns or before the people on holy days.

Again to the left of the Middle Gate, around a giant plane tree you see marble posts once used to impale heads of viziers or other important people found guilty of injustice. A large open pit visible beyond the marble posts toward the back of the Archaeological Museum marks the spot of a Byzantine cistern, which was inadvertently discovered while new electrical lines were being grounded in 1975. A number of Byzantine and Roman cisterns, some of which were also used during Ottoman

The Middle Gate

The Middle Gate inscription

times, have since been discovered within the palace grounds.

The turreted octagonal towers of the **Middle Gate** rise high above a crenellated wall. Although occasionally referred to by its Arabic name, Babüs-selam ("The Gate of Peace or Salutation"), it was most commonly called by its Turkish name, Orta Kapı ("The Middle Gate"). Historians do not all agree on the date or source of these two towers, but they seem to be more Byzantine in style than Turkish, perhaps the work of a Greek architect. They were certainly standing by 1493 when the Nuremberg chronicle was published since they appear in the woodcut print of Constantinople. They also resemble drawings of the old Cannon Gate by the Golden Horn of Byzantine date. The inscription above the Middle Gate in gold lettering is the Islamic creed, or testimony of faith: "There is no God but Allah and Mohammed is His prophet." Immediately under it is the tuğra of Sultan Mahmud II and on either side of the gateway are two more tuğra, both of Mustafa III. They all commemorate some restoration work ordered by these sultans. According to an inscription on the left door, the great iron doors

date to the time of Suleyman in the sixteenth century.

The Middle Gate

The Topkapi Museum entrance at the Middle Gate

## QUESTIONS

**8.** How does the Middle Gate differ from the Imperial Gate?

**9.** Why do you think the hospital was located at the entrance?

**10.** Who ate the bread made from coarse dark flour? The white flour?

**11.** What were the straw mats used for?

**12.** Identify the structures in the miniature painting of the first couryard. (See page 18) Which ones have disappeared?

**13.** Compare the interior of the domes with attention to the corners. How is the transition created between wall and dome of the Tiled Pavilion?

**14.** Is the roof of the Tiled Pavilion perfectly flat?

The Tower of Justice

# Second Courtyard

The official entrance to the Topkapi Museum is through the Middle Gate, which is equipped with airport style security checks and entrance turnstiles to welcome you. As at the Imperial Gate, weapons hanging from the Middle Gate's vestibule served as a reminder to those who passed to leave their weapons behind. Only members of the court and people on official visit could enter. The meeting of the Council, known as the Divan, that took place between two and four times a week, depending on the sultan, was the most important event in the second courtyard. Viziers (ministers of the sultan), the ulema (doctors of Islamic canon law), the defterdar (treasurers), and tezkereci (a secretary who wrote official decrees) met with the grand vizier to hear complaints and set right injustices as well as discuss pressing matters of the state. Functioning primarily as the high court of justice, the Divan was the supreme organ of the government. In addition to the Council meeting, other important events that took place here included the religious feast days, the accession ceremony of the new sultan, and audiences of foreign embassies with the sultan.

Horses and carriages were left in the first courtyard as complete silence was imposed here in the second. Only the sultan could enter riding a horse and ladies of the Harem might be driven through the gate in a carriage. Utterance of a mere word could prompt a thrashing with a stick. Sometimes ten thousand people gathered here for a banquet and ate their meal in complete silence. The imposition of silence served to create an aura of otherworldliness within the courtyard, with the

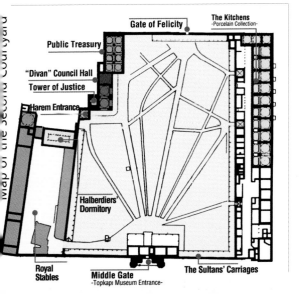

Map of the Second Courtyard

The Kitchens
-Porcelain Collection-

Gate of Felicity

Public Treasury

"Divan" Council Hall
Tower of Justice

Harem Entrance

Halberdiers'
Dormitory

Royal
Stables

Middle Gate
-Topkapı Museum Entrance-

The Sultans' Carriages

added practical benefit of making it easier to control large numbers of people within a closed space. In the sixteenth century, two mutes were introduced into the court to teach the pages sign language so that they could communicate. In time, everyone learned sign language.

Cypress motif tiles

Many of the sultans continued the practice of introducing mutes to keep up the custom of signing. Deaf mutes were also considered useful executioners and they were often employed for secret assassinations.

Although the peacocks and gazelles that once roamed freely are no longer to be found, and the many fountains that enhanced this garden of paradise have disappeared, lovely cypress trees still line the walkways as they once did in Ottoman times. Despite its name, the Italian cypress is actually native to the eastern Mediterranean region and is recognizable by its tall columnar shape and dark green color. It is by far the favorite tree of the second courtyard and seen in the miniature paintings from the early sixteenth century on. Some plane trees of huge dimensions and colorful crepe myrtle dot the courtyard among other trees.

Because the buildings of the second and third courtyards are made of stone and had lead roofs, they have survived far longer than those of the first courtyard. Though most have been renovated or rebuilt more than once, their functions hardly ever changed. When Mehmed II had the promontory cleared and terraced for the construction of the palace, a great deal of building material was uncovered and reused in its construction. Thus, all of the marble columns and many of the stone blocks you see are of spoglia or reused material. Even though marble quarries were plentiful and their locations well-known, with some as close as Marmara Island, it was still easier and less costly to reuse stone from other

Green Breccia column

Lead covered domes

buildings. When Selim I conquered Egypt, a large part of the booty he took was granite and porphyry from ancient temples, which he had shipped to Istanbul. The marble of Marmara Island was not regularly quarried until the eighteenth century and only then did stonecutters form a guild. As for the lead used for the roofs, the primary source were the mines at Banjo Lukas in Bosnia. Lead rolled into sheets lends itself to draping over surfaces to make them impervious to water. The bluish-grey patina it takes on when oxidized has become a distinctive color of the domes of Istanbul.

Fountain

Past a small fountain downhill, a path leads to the courtyard of the **Royal Stables**. A natural slope in the terrain was terraced for the stables, so that they were not visible from the second courtyard. Twenty-five or thirty of the sultan's favorite horses were kept in the stable located in this courtyard. The sultan would often go riding or hunting in the company of some chosen pages in the wooded areas surrounding the palace. A small eighteenth century masjid, or small prayer hall, and a bathhouse, built by Mahmud I's chief black eunuch, Beşir Ağa (Master Beşir), stand in the courtyard.

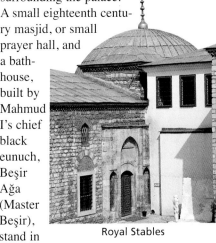

Royal Stables

Largely rebuilt in 1942, this masjid and bath were for the stable master, officers, and stable keepers who looked after the sultan's horses and lived in the dormitories of this courtyard. You might notice that one of the corners of the masjid differs from the others. This is because one of them is actually a built-in minaret, purposely built low so that it would not rise above the surrounding walls.

Sultan Osman II

The domed section of the royal stables used to hold a special treasury of horse caparisons. Bits, buckles, and stirrups made of gold and silver together with bridles and saddles embedded with precious jewels filled this

Path from stables

treasury. Today, the stables occasionally house special exhibits.

Back up the hill in the second courtyard, look for the high **Tower of Justice**. It is the highest structure of the palace and is therefore visible from a distance. You will pass the entrance to the Harem on your way to the tower. Although a tower has occupied this spot since Mehmed II's time, the present version rebuilt in the eighteenth century with neoclassical architectural elements, such as the composite capitals, is the tallest yet. The sultan used to sit in the room with glass windows on all four sides to observe his palace, city, and empire below him. Just below the Tower of Justice is the Divan or Council Hall where the viziers, as the ministers of state were called, would meet under the watchful eye of the sultan to administer

justice throughout the empire and hear cases of injustice. Because the strength and prosperity of the empire depended on the proper administration of justice, the Tower of Justice expressed a strong message to the people.

The entrance to the Harem area is in the corner below the tower. Immediately to the left of it stands the door to the dormitory for the "tressed halberdiers" whose long tresses and shaven faces were a sign of bondage that also gave them access to all parts of the palace. Among their many duties were carrying wood into

Tressed Halberdier

the Harem and third courtyard as well as washing the marble paths and columns with sponges soaked in rosewater, vinegar, and lemon juice to make them shiny and scented. The dormitory is important since it is one of the few sixteenth century buildings still intact. Having recently been restored, it is to be open for public view in the near future.

Just below the Tower of Justice is the Divan or Council Hall where the viziers (government ministers) met some-

Tower of Justice

*Dinner offered to Vicount d'Andrezel in the Divan* by J. B. Vanmour

times up to four times weekly to discuss state matters and to dispense justice as they heard grievances of the empire's subjects. "Divan" comes from the Arabic word meaning council meeting and by implication also both the room and the low couches on which the ministers sat. A wide awning supported by columns of Thessalian green breccia marble, pink basalt,

Divan

and grey proconnesian marble in grand Turkish architectural style form the triple entrance. The entrance farthest to the right, closed today, leads to what used to be

an archive. Going through the middle entrance, you come into the Divan, a double-domed room separated by a symbolic marble doorway. The room to the left was for the viziers while the one to the right was for the chancery and individuals who had petitioned the sultan. At times, the sultan sat just above the viziers behind the latticed window that you see in the wall facing the left entrance. From here, with the curtain closed, he would listen in without the council members necessarily being aware of his presence. A simple stamp on the floor from the sultan could signal an execution. Some

Marble doorway

van Colonnade

sultans actively took part in the council meetings, as in the case of Murad III, who left his lattice window and entered the chamber on at least one occassion when he saw that the petitioner had been neglected.

Golden Pendant in the Divan

Hanging from the center of the dome in the Divan is a golden pendant with a tassle at the end. According to legend, Alexander the Great had a golden globe made from the gold of his newly conquered lands, and since Mehmed II saw himself as another Alexander the Great, he similarly used his own golden pendant as a symbol of his power over the world. Subsequent sultans followed suit so that golden pendants generally came to indicate the sultan's power. Usage of pendants was most likely not so foreign to the sultans, however, as the hanging of ostrich eggs with tassels from the domes of mosques and tombs had been a popular practice since early Islamic times. This was because of the association of eggs with immortality and the holy cities of Mecca and Medina where ostriches used to be a common sight.

Bronze braziers for heating are found in the center of each room of the Divan. Although the two rooms have been remodeled and renovated many times, the present decorations date from the end of the eighteenth century, when Divan meetings ceased to be held there while the location is the same as it was when Topkapi was opened in 1478. The larger floor plan, however, is from the renovations completed during the time of Suleyman the Magnificent in the sixteenth century.

Next to the Divan stands an

eight-domed treasury building known as the **Public Treasury** where revenues from the provinces were stored in underground vaults. The janissary soldiers were paid from these revenues every three months. In a symbolic ritual, the sultan would join the 61st troop, which composed his personal bodyguard, and receive a salary only to return it with a big premium added.

Before they were paid, the coins from foreign mints were tested for their metal content.

Today, weapons and armor are displayed in the Public Treasury. Many of the weapons came to the palace as part of war booty after Ottoman victories.

The oldest pieces are the seventh century swords dating to the Umayyad period. The Umayyads were the first Muslim dynasty to rule over much of today's Syria and

Ottoman standards

Israel. They conquered most of North Africa before eventually settling in Spain. Painted Turkish shields made of wicker with steel centers served as lightweight ceremonial gear. It is interesting to compare the Ottoman Turkish, Mamluk, and Persian helmets. The Persian ones are far more fanciful, with dragons' heads curving up to the pointed tip. The Turkish swords called "yatağan" with their grooved curved steel blades that thicken toward the pommel look more deadly than the giant medieval European swords in the case on the back wall.

The "tuğ" are the tall standards topped with horsetail tufts standing in a row as you enter the Public Treasury. Originating from Central Asia, the Turkic peoples' homeland, this type of standard was a symbol of rank in the Ottoman army. Before leaving for the battlefield, the sultan would thrust two standards in the ground in front of the Middle Gate of the palace.

Public Treasury

Just outside the door stands a marble target stone, which looks like a column. First brought to the palace in the twentieth century, the stone was originally set up to commemorate a spot in Levent, a modern suburb of Istanbul, where Selim III's arrow landed. Now we are in the far left corner of the second courtyard.

Immediately on your right after passing through the Middle Gate are two models of the palace grounds and on the walls some maps showing the territory of the Ottoman Empire at different periods. Further ahead you can look through the windows to see a display of some nineteenth century carriages, most of which were made in France or Germany. Perhaps the carriage covered with diamond shaped mirrors is the most unusual.

The upper pulvinus section of an enormous Late Roman capital stands in the corner of the second courtyard. There is an opening through the colonnade to a smaller court-

yard leading to the kitchens from which you can see a giant Corinthian composite capital with faces peaking out from acanthus leaves on all four sides and a column drum. They are situated over the spots where they were discov-

Fifth century pulvinus

ered underground between 1959 and 1962 while work on the foundations was being carried out. They have been dated to the fifth century C.E. and, judging from the holes on the top of the capital, which match those of the pulvinus the two parts formed a whole which was on top of a triumphal column and bore a bronze statue, most likely of a Byzantine emperor

If you walk straight ahead toward the third gate, about half way down the path, a small fence cordons off some brickwork. This is the top of a fifth century C.E. Byzantine cistern excavated in 1968, one of many within the palace grounds. Early Byzantine remains are incorporated all over the palace, particularly the marble

Fifth century capital

Kitchen colonnade

columns and capitals of the colonnades. The light green breccia stone, Thessalian stone from the Larissa valley in Greece, and yellowish breccia columns and pink Egyptian basalt from Aswan in Egypt often indicate important structures and contrast with the more common greyish white proconnesia marble columns from Marmara Island. Stonecutters carved Ottoman style capitals from Byzantine capitals as well.

The great chimneys of the **kitchens** rise up conspicuously behind the colonnade on the right side of the courtyard. They are clearly visible even from the Sea of Marmara. Originally they had pyramidal caps over the smokestacks, but they were removed during the restoration project carried out in the 1940's. The colonnade acts as a curtain to hide the

Chimney

kitchens and creates a courtyard space on the other side. In these kitchens, food for everyone in the palace, often thousands of people, was prepared and served. Servants would stand in a long line across the courtyard and pass the dishes from one to another swiftly and in silence. Every three months, ten to fifteen thousand janissaries were fed soup, rice pilaf, and sweet zerde (a mixture of saffron, sugar, and rice) from these kitchens. One of the kitchens, for example, was used exclusively for the preparation of sweets and jams while another was reserved for making soap and medicines. Meals for the sultan and the sultan's mother were also prepared in their own separate kitchens. It is impossible to tell how most of the kitchens were used because their functions changed over the years. There were also facilities here for the cooks and their assistants including dormitories, a masjid, and a bathhouse. Up to three hundred people at a time would work in these kitchens.

Smokestacks

For the time being, the kitchens are used to exhibit the **porcelain and celadon col-**

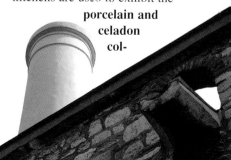

**lection** of the museum. The secret to making porcelain dishes is kaolin, white clay that produces very thin, hard, translucent pottery. The process was known only in China and later in Japan until the early eighteenth century when a German brought the technique to Europe and set up a porcelain factory. The technique quickly spread from one royal palace to another within Europe. The green celadon ware, also porcelain, was prized because it changed color when the food was poisoned, though it was hardly foolproof. Most of these particular dishes came all the way from China, placed in one another with mud between them forming long single bundles wrapped in goat hair tap-

estries for extra protection. Most made the long journey across Central Asia by

Banquet scene

camel caravans, while others came by ship. Many were first used in Egypt or Iran and after Ottoman conquests brought to Istanbul as booty in the sixteenth and seventeenth centuries. According to an eighteenth century inventory, the palace had more than twenty thou

View of Topkapı Palace from the Sea of Marmara

Baklava

sand pieces of Chinese blue and white porcelain and celadon wares, some of which were produced specifically for Ottoman usage.

Primarily the Ottoman Sultan and perhaps his mother ate from these luxurious porcelain plates and bowls. They used spoons with long handles to take the food from a dish and drank sweet fruit sherbets poured from porcelain bottles. Interestingly enough, the sultan ate from such precious dishes even while on campaign. Roses, tulips, and carnations were cut and placed in narrow necked vases for decoration. Today there are about ten thousand pieces of Chinese blue and white porcelain and celadon in the collection –though only a fraction is on display– forming one of the largest and most important porcelain collections in the world.

It is interesting to note that the first porcelain factory in Istanbul, which produced "Eseri" dishes near the Golden Horn, was established only in 1845. These locally produced glassware and porcelains of the nineteenth and twentieth centuries are on display at the end of the courtyard in the sweet beverage kitchen. In the confectioner's kitchen, pots and pans of immense dimensions are exhibited. They are made of copper with a tin interior to protect people from the poisonous effects of heated copper. On the fifteenth day of Ramadan, the fasting month in Islam, baklava was made for about fifteen thousand janissaries in this kitchen and served after sunset. Opposite the kitchens' entrances is the doorway to a small collection of Ottoman silver. Most are gifts presented to Sultan Abdulhamid II, perhaps the most notable of which is a silver model of Ahmet III's fountain; this particular gift

Kitchens

was given to him by his daughter in 1901 to commemorate his 25th year in power.

Finally, we come to the gate commonly known by the Arabic name, Babüs-saade, which means **"Gate of Felicity,"** leading to the sultan's private quarters and the royal pages' dormitories. The gate had various names: "Bab-ı Ali" (The Sublime Porte, although the name would later be trasferred to another gate; see page 17) and Gate of Petitions, but it was most often called the Gate of Felicity. On special occasions like accession ceremonies or religious feast days, a special carpet weighing 150 kilos and on it a ceremonial throne were placed just to the left of the gate for the sultan to make his appearance before the court. Even when the Ottoman sultans moved permanently to Dolmabahçe Palace, accession ceremonies and the religious feast

The Gate of Felicity

days continued to be celebrated in Topkapi Palace.

While passing through the gate, look to the ground and you will see the small marble knob that protects the spot where the holy standard

*Allegiance ceremony of Sultan Selim III* by Constantin Kapıdağlı

figures, though they are clearly reminiscent of European painting. Theoretically, Islamic law forbids the depiction of human figures since the human form is the work of Allah. Although human figures abound in Islamic miniature art, it would not have been deemed appropriate to have them depicted on a wall. In the eighteenth and nineteenth centuries, many of the white walls around the courtyard were painted with linear perspective frescoes of landscapes which can be seen in the nineteenth century photographs taken of them before the palace became a museum. European style landscape painting was introduced to the Ottoman Empire during the reign of Selim III. Later, it was a course of study in the new military schools since they needed accurate sketches of battlegrounds for military use; however, most of the Topkapi murals are of imaginary landscapes.

was placed during the ceremony that took place just prior to going to war. The holy standard was a symbol of the Ottoman claim to the Caliphate as the leader of Islam for it is believed to have been carried by the Prophet Mohammed and came to Istanbul with other holy objects after Selim I's conquest of Egypt. The last time it was shown to the public was in 1914 when the Ottoman Army went to fight in the First World War. It is now kept in a silver box in the Holy Relics room of the Privy Chamber in the third courtyard.

Passage through this gate was controlled by a eunuch known as "Kapı Ağa" (Master of the Gate). His proximity to the sultan often made him extremely powerful. The royal pages would try very hard to win his favor because their assignments were in his hands. Khadim Hasan Pasha was a eunuch who entered the palace as a child through the "devşirme" levy system of Christian children to be trained for posts in the palace. He eventually rose to the rank of Master of the Gate, then Chief

Tuğra

Standing just under the canopy before the gateway and looking up, you can see eighteenth century Romantic period frescoes on either side. You will notice that these paintings do not contain human

Pendant at the Gate of Felicity

Treasurer of the Inner Palace, Governor of Anatolia and Egypt, and finally Grand Vizier in 1597. Only one year later he was executed on charges of corruption, a common scenario for grand viziers.

Inside the Gate of Felicity are waiting areas to the left and right where foreign ambassadors sat before entering the Chamber of Petitions or the Audience Hall, a building which cleverly blocks the view of the private quarters of the third courtyard from this vantage point. The sultan was just barely visible from here as he sat on his throne in the far left-hand corner of the Audience Hall. From this gate, foreign ambassadors would watch as the gifts they brought to the sultan were carried into the Hall.

## QUESTIONS

**15.** What were the conditions for entering through the Middle Gate?

**16.** Why would there be a treasury near the stables?

**17.** Can you identify the room and the various figures in the painting by Vanmour (page 35)?

**18.** Why do you suppose Sultan Mahmud II made the Tower of Justice taller?

**19.** Why are the kitchen chimneys so tall?

**20.** Besides porcelains, what else do you think came by camel caravans across Central Asia?

**21.** What is going on in the miniature of the banquet scene (page 40)?

**22.** In the painting by Constantin Kapıdağlı (page 42), how is the Gate of Felicity different from the one you see today? Are any of the figures in the painting recognizable?

The Gate of Felicity colonnade

# Third Courtyard

Through the Gate of Felicity we enter into the inner section of the palace. This area, which includes the Harem section, was strictly for the sultan, his family, and members of his household. Household members included the male and female slaves selected to be educated in the palace and the eunuchs who supervised and guarded the dormitories of both the Harem women and male pages. Within the inner section of the palace, male and female quarters were clearly segregated. All female family and household members as well as young princes lived in the Harem section. Even within the Harem section, segregation between male and females was the rule. During later centuries, adult royal princes remained in the Harem as hostages of their sultan brother. Only the sultan had free access to all areas of the palace.

The first building encountered in the third courtyard after entrance through the Gate of Felicity is the **Chamber of Petitions** (Arz Odası), also known as the Audience Hall, used for private audiences with the sultan. This building dates from the sixteenth century, apparently rebuilt on the same spot where the original fifteenth century structure

stood, but enlarged. It has, however, undergone many renovations since the sixteenth century. The fountain in the wall to the right of

Chamber of Petitions

the door bears Suleyman the Magnificent's monogram, thus dating this particular structure to the sixteenth century. This is a typical lead-roofed Ottoman pavilion with a colonnade and broad eaves all the way around it. Here again, the columns selected for the colonnade are of different types and colors of stone. There are two sections: the main section where the throne is located on the left and to the right, a small prayer room with an ablution fountain and latrine. The sultan would receive ambassadors and officials of the state in the Chamber of Petitions, but he neither spoke nor even looked at the foreign ambassadors, for it would be below him to address another person or to be addressed by them. Any dialogue would take place between inter-preters while the ambassadors waited under the vestibule of the Gate of Felicity. The sultan usual-ly sat cross-legged, motionless and silent on his throne while his viziers stood in respect with their hands clasped before them. The throne that you see now was ordered by Mehmed III in 1597, and though most of the jewels are now lost, it was once gilt and cov-ered with precious stones. Descriptions of the room as it looked tell us that it had gold-plated walls studded with jew-els and a silver fireplace. The floors were covered with car-pets of silk, gold, and silver threads studded with jewels. In the mid-nineteenth century, the gold and jewels were sold to help finance the construction of Dolmabahçe Palace, the new Ottoman imperial residence.

The doors around the Chamber of Petitions had specific functions: the door to the left of the latticed

window was reserved for the sul-tan, while the door to the right could be used by anyone. To the rear another door was known as the Gate of Punishment since judges found guilty of injustice exited from this door and were executed under the vestibule of the Gate of Felicity. The large latticed window was for the sultan to watch gifts, slaves, and even heads of traitors paraded in front of him on the porch.

In the left corner of the courtyard is the exit of the Harem sec-tion known as the **Aviary**. The small two-story eighteenth century building, (the balcony, however, being a nineteenth century addition) facing

"Aviary"

the courtyard looks like a tradi-tional Mediterranean aviary and probably is responsible for the name given to the gate. Although it has been assumed that the sul-tans' favorite food, quail and pheasant, was cooked in the small kitchen while the birds were raised in the lower floor of the building, this appears to be fantasy. It is, however possible that the name originates from the ritual of feeding your beloved some roasted quail on the first night together. If the woman ate the bird, she accepted the man's love. If she did not, well then, the story ended there. There is a saying in Turkish that reflects this ritual: "Not every bird should be eaten."

The building at an obvious

Throne in the Chamber of Petitions

angle is a **mosque** and though what you see today dates mostly to nineteenth century remodeling, we know that there had been a mosque in this very spot as far back as the time of Mehmed II. Unlike the other structures, it is aligned so that it faces Mecca. The eunuchs and royal pages from each of the different sections of the palace prayed in the mosque together four times a day with the last evening prayer taking place in their dormitories. Although they prayed together, the royal pages sat in special sections according to which parts of the palace they had been assigned to and even entered the mosque by rank: according to a seventeenth century description, first Privy Chamber pages, followed by those of the Treasury, the Commissary, the Falconers, and finally the Expeditionary Force pages. Today the mosque houses the library of Topkapi Palace Museum.

Harem exit

The left colonnade continues on the other side of the mosque and the first doorway leads to the **dormitory for the Privy**

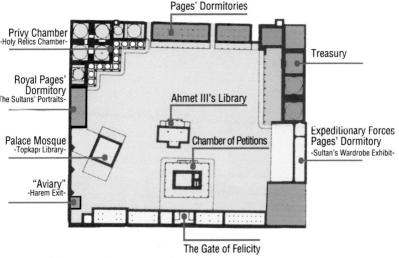

Privy Chamber
-Holy Relics Chamber-

Pages' Dormitories

Treasury

Royal Pages'
Dormitory
-The Sultans' Portraits-

Ahmet III's Library

Palace Mosque
-Topkapı Library-

Chamber of Petitions

Expeditionary Forces
Pages' Dormitory
-Sultan's Wardrobe Exhibit-

"Aviary"
-Harem Exit-

The Gate of Felicity

Map of the Third Courtyard

Sultan Mehmed II

Sultan Selim II

**Chamber or Royal Pages**. Today, the former dormitory houses a permanent exhibition of the **portraits of the sultans**. The restoration of this building was completed in 2000. According to the account of a pageboy who lived in the palace in the seventeenth century, fifteen to twenty pages slept in this dormitory with torches kept lighted all night so that the white eunuch in charge could watch over them and presumably keep them out of mischief. Some of their lessons also took place in the dormitory.

A copy of the famous portrait of Mehmed II by Gentile Bellini (the original is in the National Gallery in London) is on display here. The Venetian artist's stay in Istanbul in the 1470's is well documented because he was sent by the Venetian Doge, but no other works composed by him while in the service of Mehmed II have

survived. Mehmed II's son, Beyazid, was a conservative and religious man. Since portraiture is forbidden by Islamic law, Beyazid did his utmost to dispose of any portraits in the palace, including the aforementioned portrait of his father, which was auctioned off and thus made its way from Istanbul to Venice, and finally to London. The "Veronese School" portraits of the sultans are also copies of a series produced by a group of Italian artists influenced by Paolo Veronese in Venice. Copies were painted and sent to Istanbul to be used as examples for paintings for a book of miniatures about the lives of the Ottoman sultans upon the request of Nakkaş Osman, the court miniaturist, and Lokman, the author of the book, during the sultanate of Murad III. It is particularly interesting to compare the seventeenth century Italian realism

Sultan Abdulhamid

in oil on canvas of the "Veronese School" series with the Turkish miniature portraits by Nakkaş Osman, displayed in the glass cases, with their vivid mineral colors and gold on paper. As different as they are in size, style, and medium, there is a similarity detectable in the facial features of the sultans. In the eighteenth century, a painter of Armenian origin named Rafael reversed the miniature style by portraying Abdulhamid I in what seems to be a giant miniature, or rather a life-size portrait with stylistic qualities of a miniature: attention to details, vivid colors, solid background, and seated static pose.

At the far left hand corner of the first section of the third courtyard there is a doorway to the **Holy Relics Chamber**. Composed of an entrance area, bedroom, and throne room of the sultan, the **Privy Chamber** (Has

Odası) was located here until Murad III moved his to the Harem. Once again, the colorful stone columns in the corner of the courtyard immediately draw one's attention. The doorway is decorated with tiles and on either side are what look like a sultan's monogram, but are actually verses in praise of Sultan Ahmet III - an expert calligrapher who designed them himself!

In the center of the first room you step into is a fountain, its marble basin probably carved in the eighteenth century, while its upper water spout dates to the fourth century of the early Byzantine era and is made of Thessalian green breccia stone. Mehmed II certainly used this area as his private quarters and it has been suggested that he employed Gentile Bellini not just to paint his portrait, but to fresco the walls of his bedroom with erotic scenes as well, and that mosaicists probably decorated the floors. If there ever had been figurative scenes

Privy Chamber colonnade

Privy Chamber entrance

here, however, Mehmed's son Beyazid, known to be particularly pious and conservative, would most certainly have had them destroyed. During the reign of Suleyman, Persian silk carpets and leopard skins are said to have covered the floor of this room where the sultan would sit on a throne with crystal lions on each side, like the Biblical King Solomon. He slept in a canopied gilt bed on three mattresses of cotton and feathers that were rolled up during the day. Murad III had a new Privy Chamber built in the Harem, though the old Privy Chamber continued to be used by the sultan for private prayer or occasionally for private audiences.

The first holy relics were brought as booty to Istanbul after Selim I's conquest of Egypt in 1517. Taken from the Mamluk treasury in Cairo, the most important relics to have found their way to Istanbul were the Prophet Mohammed's Blessed Mantle, holy standard, sword, and bow. They are now kept behind a glass door in what once was the Throne Room to the right after the entrance atrium. The mantle is kept in the large gold box, while the standard is in the silver box. The legend behind the mantle is that through a poem he wrote in his honor, the poet, Kaab bin Zuheyr asked the Prophet Mohammed's forgiveness for not immediately turning to Islam. The poem begins with the words: "The world receives abundance of light from our Prophet…" Prophet Mohammed was so moved that he gave his cloak to Kaab who kept it until his death, when it then passed on to the caliphs and through inheritance to the Ummayads, the Abbasids, and finally the Mamluks in Egypt until it was taken by Selim.

During Ramadan the Prophet's mantle, said to be made of black wool with a cream colored interior, would be taken out of its gold box and dipped in rosewater, which was considered to have healing powers. According to eighteenth and nineteenth century descriptions, while only the sultan was permitted to actually touch the Blessed Mantle, the family members were allowed to sniff a small piece of muslin cloth placed on the mantle on the fifteenth day of

Ramadan. They would then keep the muslin as special protection. A few of the sultans wore the mantle into battle believing it would guarantee victory. It is known, for example, that Mehmed III wore it to battle against the Hapsburgs in 1596.

As sultans had renovations commissioned in Mecca and Medina, they would bring back objects to Istanbul thereby adding to the number of holy relics. Today, some pilgrims come to visit and pray before the relics here, where the Koran is recited aloud by a hafiz (a person who has memorized the entire Koran) all day long. The general population, however, does not know that the mantle is kept in Topkapi Palace nor do most Muslims associate Topkapi Palace with the Prophet Mohammed. Since the foundation of the Turkish Republic, the mantle has not been taken out of the gold box for viewing.

There is another mantle in Istanbul that is also believed to have been worn by the Prophet Mohammed. Ahmet I had it brought to Istanbul from Cairo in the seventeenth century. The Hırka-ı Şerif (Holy Mantle) Mosque was built especially for it in the nineteenth century and it continues to be displayed there today during Ramadan for public viewing.

There is a long rod labeled as the "Rod of Moses" in one of the display cases in the room to the left of the entrance. This is believed to be the same rod of Moses that is mentioned in the Book of Ceremonies written by the Byzantine Emperor Constantine VII in the ninth century. According to the Book of Ceremonies, the rod was brought (together with a relic of the True Cross) by Constantine the Great from Jerusalem to Constantinople where it was then kept in a special chapel in the Grand Palace of the Byzantine Emperors. In the same glass case that holds the rod, a sword believed to have been the one with which King David beheaded Goliath, is also displayed. There is writing, apparently in Assyrian and Arabic, on one side. It was miraculously discovered in the inner treasury in 1696 during the sultanate of Mustafa II who carried it on campaigns in the Balkans to ensure victory. In the glass case behind it, there is a white turban said to be that of Joseph, the handsome son of Jacob and Rachel who was

Library of Sultan Ahmet III

sold as a slave and became the officer of the Egyptian Pharaoh!

Just behind the Audience Hall is the **Ahmet III's Library** built by Ahmet III in the eighteenth century. Ahmet III was the sultan of the "Tulip Period," so called because of the general intense interest

Library interior

in tulips, manifested not only in the terraced gardens of the third courtyard, but in the designs of fabrics and ceramic tiles as well. The library is a graceful structure with large windows and low divans for reading. The substructure is high with windows to permit constant airflow to protect the manuscripts in the cupboards from the dangers of humidity. The 3,515 volumes that used to be stored here are now in the mosque just to the right of the library. Ahmet III was an accomplished calligrapher and bibliophile, so it is only fitting that he should have built a library for himself and the royal pages. The sultan himself also wrote the inscriptions just above the doorway to the Privy Chamber.

As you pass through the third gate and walk to the right, in the first corner there is a small courtyard behind the wall where the furnace for the large bath was located. In the fifteenth century, there was a giant aviary housing the sultan's birds in this corner. Later, in the seventeenth century as the furnace for the Imperial Bath replaced the aviary, it was rebuilt as a freestanding structure. Pigeons with pearl anklets performed acrobatics in flight at the sound of a whistle while nightingales and canaries sang to enhance this garden of paradise.

The first doorway on the right leads to the exhibition room of the **Sultan's Wardrobe**. The room was originally a dormitory for the pageboys of the Expeditionary Forces. One of their duties was to look after the sultan's wardrobe. The reason we can see the caftans (outer robes) and uniforms today

Expeditionary Forces Pages' Dormitory

is that any piece of clothing worn by a sultan was preserved after his death; after being wrapped up in bundles, the clothing would be placed in the inner treasury vaults by the crown prince or grand vizier with the sultan's name attached. However, when the palace was turned into a museum, questions began to arise about which

Silk Caftan

decorative flaps lying to the side. Most are made of silk with floral or geometric designs. Istanbul and Bursa were the main production centers for the sultan's silks, but some came from Italy and Spain as well. Çatma, Seraser, Hatayi, and Kemha are a few names used to describe the fabrics, of which there are about 650 different types in all. Of these, Seraser was the

Mehmed or Ahmed a bundle belonged to since nametags lacked the appropriate "I," "II," etc. The clothing is displayed in chronological order starting from the right. A caftan was worn with an inner tunic and baggy shalvar pants that were narrow at the ankle. Some of the caftans have very long sleeves that are not really sleeves since the sultan did not put his arms through them, but rather they served as

most valuable since gold and silver threads were woven with silk to create it. Hatayi comes from Cathay, the word for China, and describes Chinese designs. One of the most common patterns is the

Entrance to Sultan's Wardrobe Exhibit

"triple ball-double band" known as "chitamani" that appears to be of Buddhist origin. It was originally thought to signify the earth and sea or three pearls and the waves, but later interpreted as the spots of the leopard and stripes of the tiger to represent the courage and strength of the sultan. Tulip patterns were also favored because

Wardrobe Exhibit

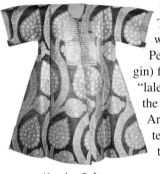

Kemha Caftan

the Turkish word (of Persian origin) for tulip, "lale," uses the same Arabic letters as those used for Allah, thus giving it a symbolic meaning. There is a very marked rupture in fashion in the nineteenth century with the introduction of European style military uniforms replacing the caftans. Selim III was the first sultan to introduce European style drills and troops. The janissaries and the religious leaders who finally overthrew Selim III were fiercely opposed to these drastic changes. In 1826, Mahmud II abolished the janissary corps in a great blood bath and introduced new uniforms as well as European style drills for his "New Order" troops. Mahmud II is invariably portrayed in fitted uniform donning a red fez, which is a brimless hat made of felt produced in the city of Fez, Morocco. This type of hat became the new headgear for the modern Ottoman male subject, regardless of his religious or ethnic background, when Mahmud II decided to modernize society and do away with the turban. Ironically enough, a century later Mustafa

Kemal would ban the fez in favor of the European bowler hat as the proper attire for the new Turkish republican male subject.

Mahmud II disbanded the janissary corps to replace them with troops of free men who soon became the new educated elite at a time when the institution of royal pages was waning. Considering this historical context, it is not surprising that the founders of modern Turkey should come from the military schools of the empire.

Exiting the imperial wardrobe exhibition room, continue down some stairs to the right through an arched colonnade to the **Treasury** display rooms. (Please note that a separate ticket must be purchased for entrance into this section at the ticket booth in front of the Middle

Private Treasury-Imperial Bath

Gate.) It is possible that the architect of this colonnade was an Italian employed by Sultan Mehmed II as the composite capitals and rounded arches recall Italian renaissance porticoes. In contrast, the doorways, windows, and wall moldings are specifically Islamic in style: muqarnas (or stalactite motif) molding and pointed arched upper windows are examples of the like. Looking at the Treasury section from the middle of the third courtyard is a good way to begin since it offers a view of the colonnade and the domes of the original bath. Today precious objects are beautifully displayed in the Treasury, the most famous being the Spoonmaker's Diamond and the

emerald Topkapi Dagger, both possibly Indian in origin. Many romantic legends surround these objects in particular. According to one such legend, the exquisite diamond is called "Spoonmaker's Diamond" because it was sold for two spoons to a spoonmaker after being retrieved from the rubbish outside the palace grounds by a fisherman. However, the origin of the name may simply be the spoon-like shape of this tear-drop diamond, which is one of the largest cut diamonds in the world.

In 1746, the "Topkapi Dagger" was chosen by Mahmud I together with many other gifts to be presented to Nadir Shah, the Afghan conqueror of India and usurper of

Capital

Treasury Exhibit entrances

the Persian Throne, after a peace treaty was signed between the two rulers. The dagger is delicately decorated with colorful enamel work in the design of a fruit basket, set with three cabochon emeralds on the sheath and another emerald at the tip with an English watch in the pommel. However, Nadir was assassinated soon after the caravan carrying gifts for him set out, and so the caravans returned without delivering the goods, and thus did the precious dagger end up back in the Ottoman Treasury.

A very beautiful golden cradle encrusted with jewels is another highlight of this section. There must have been many of these precious cradles since every child of the sultan was given three: one for everyday use from the Mint, and two magnificent cradles, one from the Valide (Queen Mother) and one from the Grand Vizier.

**Topkapi Dagger**

Of the thrones kept in the Treasury, one is known as the Bayram Throne since it was used for the sultan during the religious feasts of the Muslim calendar. It is made of walnut plated in solid gold and encrusted with peridots and olivines, either made in Egypt or by an Egyptian artisan in Istanbul. Tradition says that it was a gift from the Grand Vizier, Ibrahim Pasha, to Murad III in 1585; however, this throne does not appear in the palace registers until the end of the seventeenth century. It appears to be the same throne that Selim III is sitting on in Constantin Kapıdağlı's painting depicting the allegiance ceremony at Selim's accession in 1789. The painting is now on exhibit with the Sultans' portraits (see page 41).

Most of the objects in the Treasury were gifts. An exception is the piece of skull or occiput of Saint John the Baptist that was taken from the Church of Saint John in the Mangana Palace shortly after the conquest of Constantinople. Mehmed II presented this relic to his father's Christian wife, Mara, princess of Serbia, who in turn gave it to the monks on Mount Athos where it was kept until an Ottoman admiral stole it in the eighteenth century when the monks abandoned the monestary in an attempt to escape the plague. The relic returned to the Imperial Treasury when all of the admiral's belongings were turned over to the sultan upon his death. Centuries earlier, during the Fourth Crusaders' occupation of Constantinople in 1246, another piece of John the Baptist's skull was sent to Paris and kept in the Sainte Chapelle until being destroyed during the French Revolution.

The building that houses the first part of the Treasury used to be the large imperial hamam (bath house) described as having multi-colored marble pavement, a large central marble pool, and white marble basins with golden water spouts. The plaster paint was scented with saffron and musk. The furnaces heated the running water all through the day and night. With one of the adjacent rooms used as a music room, the imperial bath became a center for relaxation and entertainment. The rooms in the far corner were built as a private pavilion for Sultan Mehmed II. It was customary for the sultan to bathe here with his male pages on Fridays, but he certainly came on other days as well. After two violent earthquakes, Sultan Selim II had major renovations carried out in 1574. Selim II also slipped on the floor and died in the bath, in a drunken bliss, or so they say. It thereafter became known as Selim's Bath; however, whether the name was inspired by the circumstances of his death or the renovations he had carried out is hard to tell.

Çemberlitaş Bath

The first two rooms of today's Treasury exhibition section were part of the large Imperial Bath (Selim's Bath), while the last rooms in the corner were originally conceived as a private pavilion for Mehmed II. However, being a collector of a variety of holy relics and valuable ephemera, Mehmed II used these rooms as an inner treasury in which he displayed his precious Korans, Byzantine manuscripts, maps, etc. His son, Beyazid, gave most of the relics away in return for favors from Christian powers, in particular to keep his brother Cem from returning to threaten his position. In time, these two rooms of the Treasury became a depot for precious objects no longer used together with the sultan's clothing as well as archival documents and manuscripts.

Under this building are the foundations of a fourth century baptistery. This early baptistery's marble font, now located in the tulip garden, was removed when the land was cleared for the palace's construction and used by Mehmed II and subsequent sultans as a repository for gold coins in the inner treasury.

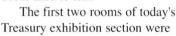

## QUESTIONS

23. Compare the portrait of Sultan Abdulhamid I by the artist Rafael (p. 51) and the one of Sultan Selim II by Nakkaş Osman (p. 50, right). (Think about how the Sultan is dressed, how he is seated, etc.)
24. Why do you suppose Sultan Selim I kept the holy relics in his Privy Chamber?
25. Why is the big diamond called the "Spoonmaker's Diamond"?
26. Looking at the Treasury from the outside, what betrays its original function as a bath?

Iftar Canopy on the Marble Terrace

# Terraced Gardens

Several passageways lead to the terrace gardens of the third courtyard. Although it seems as if we are passing to a fourth courtyard, what we encounter here is in fact a continuation of the third. Rather than the inward looking buildings of the other courtyards and the

Mecidiye Pavilion

first half of this one, here we find individual pavilions with splendid views of the Sea of Marmara and the Golden Horn. On the right, you will see three cream-colored buildings that look very different from any others you have seen so far. One of them is a small masjid looking over the Sea of Marmara. Another, which today serves as a gift shop, is the smallest of the three and was originally built to house Abdulmecid's wardrobe. The third and largest is the **Mecidiye Pavilion**; built by Abdulmecid in the 1850's, it is now used as the museum restaurant and cafeteria. An "a la carte" meal at Konyalı Restaurant is well worth it, if you have the time.

Mecidiye Pavilion is a creation of the famous Armenian architect Sarkis Balyan and is immediately recognizable as such by the Empire style reliefs. The Balyan family of architects designed most of the Ottoman palaces on the Bosphorus including Dolmabahçe, Beylerbeyi, and Çırağan Palaces. The pavilion was used in the early nineteenth century for receptions and as a place for the sultan to relax. Underneath the structure, fifteenth century barrel vaults of another pavilion were found, proof that a pavilion had been built on this very spot, probably in Mehmed II's time. Foundations of a fifth century baptistry have been excavated between Mecidiye

View of the Sea of Marmara and Asia

Pavilion and the masjid. The font was used to collect water in the palace during the Ottoman period.

As you walk away from the Sea of Marmara toward the Golden Horn, you come to a high white tower standing between terraced gardens. The **Head Physician's Tower**, the foundations of which are early Byzantine, seems to have been part of a series of towers with interconnecting arches forming an enclosure around the garden. Located just behind the Head Physician's Tower is a marble throne that was used by the sultan to watch sporting events taking

Baptismal Font

place in the garden. Originally a bishop's seat, the throne dates to around the sixth century and is made of high quality pure white marble reused from a Byzantine church.

The Head Physician's Tower seems an appropriate location to touch upon the topic of Ottoman physicians. One of the physician's duties was to make medicine. If the sultan wanted someone poisoned, it was again the head physician who concocted the necessary ingredients under the sultan's supervision. A Jewish doctor named Domenico Hierosalemitano, who resided in

this tower in the sixteenth century, wrote about life in the palace and Istanbul during the reign of Murad III after retiring and settling in a monastery in Rome. Although some salient bits about the Harem are attributed to him, it seems that most of his text was rewritten to titillate European readers, so one wonders how reliable the information really is.

Selim II seems to have been the first sultan to have a keen interest in tulips, for it is known that he ordered fifty thousand tulip bulbs from Aleppo in Syria to be planted

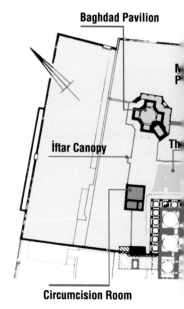

**Baghdad Pavilion**

**İftar Canopy**

**Circumcision Room**

Map of Terraced Gardens

in these gardens. Ahmet III, known as the sultan of the "Tulip Period" because his reign coincided with the peak of the tulip craze, had many hybrids of tulips created in these gardens. As you continue through the garden before climbing the steps, on the left you can see a fifth century Byzantine clover shaped **baptismal font** that was originally found under Mehmed II's treasury and later used to store the sultan's gold coins. Two lovely, white eighteenth century wooden pavilions for viewing games played in the terraced garden below and for enjoying the colors of the tulip gardens were built by Sultan Mustafa III. It is said that the disastrous decision to attack Catherine the Great's Russia was made in one of these pavilions. Further up, an elaborate tiered marble fountain stands in the garden below the Baghdad Pavilion.

Climbing up some steps, you reach the **Marble Terrace**, which is, in fact, an extension of the the Privy Chamber, now the Holy Relics Chamber. When you reach this terrace, the natural thing to do is head straight for the gilt-

İftar Canopy

bronze canopy where you can take in a dazzling view of the Golden Horn. The purpose of this court yard is to enjoy the panoramic vistas, for the surface is raised on arches seven meters above the ground. The gilt-bronze canopy was built in 1640 by Ibrahim I as a pavilion for breaking the fast during the holy month of Ramadan and a throne was placed under it

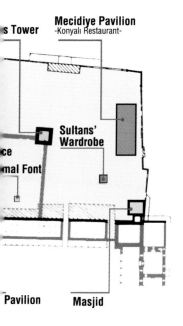

**s Tower**  **Mecidiye Pavilion** -Konyalı Restaurant-

**Sultans' Wardrobe**

ce

mal Font

**Pavilion**    **Masjid**

The Marble Pool

have the girls from the Harem perform in musical and theatrical events or play games like trying to catch the fish with nets while he sat in a boat in the middle of the pool. The Marble Terrace was more often used for pleasurable activities, though religious ceremonies took place here as well. The corpse of the sultan was washed here before being brought to his mausoleum for burial. This ritual continued even after the sultans moved to Dolmabahçe Palace.

for the sultan to use on certain festive occasions. It is known from miniatures that a throne was brought to the courtyard on occasion long before the canopy was built.

Erivan Pavilion

Poor Ibrahim was known as "Deli" or Crazy Ibrahim probably because he was mentally ill. It was Ibrahim's mental infirmity that saved him from being murdered by his sultan brother, Murad IV, and ultimately his reign and progeny that saved the Ottoman line from extinction, for all of his brothers died childless.

According to the miniatures by Levni depicting the reign of Ahmet III, royal pages used to congratulate the sultan on religious holidays as well as receive gold coins from him on the Marble Terrace. Buffoons and musicians entertained the sultan around the marble pool. The circumcision of princes sometimes took place here, after which the young princes would take their rest in the pavilions while festivities took place in the courtyard. It is also said that the sultan would close the marble courtyard off and

As you stand under the golden canopy, with your back to the Golden Horn, the **Baghdad Pavilion** is to

Circumcision ceremony

your left, while the **Erivan Pavilion** is directly in front of you. These two pavilions were built to commemorate Murad IV's victories in the east (today's Iraq and Armenia) between 1635 and 1638. By the time these pavilions were completed, however, the Ottomans had already lost Baghdad and Erivan. The two octagonal structures with their wide awnings and high surrounding colonnade mirror one another and almost outdo one another with their splendid tile and opus sectile marble decorations. Similar structures certainly stood here prior to them. Reused sixteenth century tiles decorating the Baghdad

Baghdad Pavilion

Turban

Pavilion probably came from a building standing on the same spot. Ancient marble and porphyry columns were sliced lengthwise to produce the rectangular designs while slicing columns across created the roundels of the facing of the Erivan Pavilion.

The sultan could use these two pavilions in a variety of ways; for reading, eating, listening to music, with or without the company of pages, and even sleeping. For a time, the built-in cupboards in the walls of the Erivan Pavilion were used to store the sultan's turbans, which a royal page had the specific duty of caring for.

The larger of the two, the Baghdad Pavilion, is decorated on the interior with beautiful tiles and an inscription of the Ayet al Kursi (Throne Verse) from the Koran circles the interior of the room: "Allah. There is no God but Him, the Living, the Eternal. Neither slumber, nor sleep overtakes Him. His is what is in the heavens and what is in the earth. Who can intercede with Him

on the Marble Terrace

Tile inscription

Baghdad Pavilion-interior

called bedroom of Murad III in the Harem section. The Holy Mantle had been stored here for safekeeping in the eighteenth century. There is a fireplace covered in bronze and low divan couches in niches for sitting. A formidable library of 360 volumes in the room attached to it shows that the pavilion served as a reading room. Braziers in the center were for added heat. The tiles on the walls are mainly blue and white with floral patterns. The walnut cupboards are inlaid with mother of pearl.

except by His permission. He knows what is before them and what lies behind them, and they can grasp only that part of His knowledge that He wills. His throne embraces the heavens and the earth and it tires Him not to uphold them both. His is the High, the Tremendous." (The Holy Koran, 2:255. Al Baqara, Ayet al Kursi) It is believed that those who recite this verse with sincerity are preserved from all disasters for it is the holiest verse of the holiest chapter of the Koran. The verse, in elaborate Arabic calligraphy, surrounds the throne room of the Privy Chamber where the Holy Mantle is now kept and the so-

Circumcision Chamber facade

The **Circumcision Chamber**, as it is called today, stands opposite the Erivan Pavilion. It is made up of a large room and a small bath built in the sixteenth

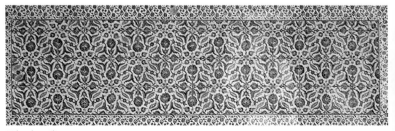

Tile detail

century and renovated in the seventeenth century. A Persian ceramicist named Habib made most of the tiles surrounding the doorway of the building. After Selim I conquered Tabriz, he sent expert artisans like Habib back to Istanbul to work in the palace workshops. When the pavilion was renovated in the seventeenth century, the tiles were reused. There is a small bath in the room that was used for ablutions, shaving, and, on occasion, royal circumcisions. When Mehmed III became sultan in 1595, it is believed he ordered his nineteen young brothers to be circumcised in this room before being strangled to death. Many of them were infants. Circumcision is a passage to manhood for the Muslim male; therefore, since a prince who posed a threat to the sultan's position had to be considered an adult, making sure the princes got circumcised served

Tile detail

to legitimize Mehmed III's order. The legitimate practice of fratricide ceased after Mehmed III, however, due to his shock at witnessing nineteen tiny coffins being brought to their mausoleum in Haghia Sophia. His son, Ahmet I, did not have his brother executed when he ascended in 1603.

Beautiful ceramic tiles are displayed on the wall of the portico that leads from the Circumcision Room to the Erivan Pavilion. Actually, this wall belongs to the Holy Relics Chamber, originally the Privy Chamber of the sultan. The marble facing was made with colorful marbles from Egypt, reused and cut to cover the lower part of the wall and make the fountain in the floor, which flowed into the marble pool. Next to the fountain is a long poem in Ottoman by Izzet Molla Keçicezade praising Mahmud II's restoration works of the Holy Relics Chamber in the early nineteenth century. Mahmud

Opus sectile detail

II's "tuğra" is located above it.

In winter, when the trees have lost their leaves, from the Marble Terrace you can see the Goths' Column in Gülhane Park near the tip of the promontory. The Goths' Column is so-called because of the inscription carved into it: "Fortunae, Reduci ob, Devictos Gothos," which means "Give thanks to Goddess Fortuna for the victory over the Goths." The inscription does not clarify in whose honor or when the column may have been erected; besides, it is likely that the column itself pre-dates the inscription. Several emperors have been proposed as possible commissioners for the triumphal column: Aurelius Claudius Gothicus (267-270) or Theodosius (I 379-395) or even Constantine the Great. Various descriptions tell of the legendary founder of the city King Byzas' golden statue gracing the capital or the statue of Saint Simon the Stylite in keeping with his hermit's life on a column, so perhaps it could be one of these. Archaeologists and historians generally date the monolithic blue veined marble column and Corinthian capital to the fourth century C.E.

The Goths' Column

## QUESTIONS

27. Walk all the way around the Mecidiye Pavilion: Do you see any differences among the four sides of this rectangular building?
28. What did people do on the "Marble Terrace"?
29. How many different floral designs do you see on the tiles of the Baghdad Pavilion?
30. How is the Mecidiye Pavilion different from the Baghdad and Erivan Pavilions? How are they similar?
31. In what ways do the conquests of the sultans play an important role in their buildings?

# Royal Pages

Generally speaking, boys aged about seven or eight were chosen from the slave markets or the local Christian populations for their good looks and intelligence to become slaves of the sultan. Until the sixteenth century, children from farming families, with the exception of only sons, were taken as levy or payment from conquered Christian populations, especially those in the Balkans. This could be seen as a cruel practice that forcibly took the brightest children from their families and depleted the regions of the most promising youth, or as an interesting way of integrating poor Christians into the Ottoman ruling class. Armenians and Jews were exempted. Muslims could not be enslaved, but in time these rules were bent. By the seventeenth century, many boys from Bosnian Muslim families entered into the palace school as royal pages, but by then the levy system had ceased to exist. At first, the young novices lived in the outer courtyard dormitories and ran errands or carried wood for the royal pages of the inner courtyard. The boys also converted to Islam upon entrance and were given new names. Their relations with the outside world were cut, though there were exceptions to this rule as well.

When a boy entered the inner palace, he would stand alone in silence for three days, after which the head white eunuch announced his entrance and inclusion into the elite class of royal pages. At puberty, the boy would be assigned to one of the chambers: Privy Chamber, Treasury, Commissary, Falconers, Expeditionary Forces, and, finally the small and large chambers. Living in dormitories of about fifteen to twenty per room in the third courtyard and closely monitored by the white eunuchs in charge, they received their education. By the end of the sixteenth century, Ibrahim's Palace, located on the Hippodrome, served as an extention of the Palace School. Their capabilities and temperaments were noted by the white eunuchs so that they could place them in the most suitable chamber. If they proved to be talented, they would be placed in service in the Privy Chamber, closest to the sultan, but during their adolescence their assignment to the various chambers could change. They all received a wage determined by the chamber to which they had been assigned, the Privy Chamber pages being the highest wage earners. So long as they were in the palace, they were not permitted to grow a beard; a shaven face was a sign of bondage. They learned to speak Ottoman Turkish and behave in the most polished manner. The royal pages in time became valiant warrior statesmen and loyal Muslims. The palace education's fundamental aim was to instill complete obedience and loyalty to the sultan. To die in the sultan's service was the greatest blessing.

The best royal pages became the viziers of the future; less talented ones found a low-ranking position in the army. By the age of about twenty-five, they were ready to leave the palace to assume responsible positions, marry, and grow a beard. Often they married the girls who had grown up very much like them, in the Harem, or even the daughters of the sultan. Over the centuries the number of royal pages varied: in 1475 there were 350 pages and by 1600 there were close to 700 of them. They never forgot they were slaves, for no matter how much wealth and property they amassed, their children could not inherit it because it was ultimately returned to the sultan.

By the nineteenth century, however, the royal pages' only duty was to look after the holy relics, for the new elite was being formed from Muslim Turkish boys at the European style military schools on the Bosphorus.

One rather extraordinary example of a page's life is that of Ibrahim, also known by the epithet "Makbul" ("The Favorite"). Suleyman the Magnificent's favorite pageboy, Ibrahim was born in the Adriatic coastal town of Parga in what is now Greece around 1493 and entered the palace school as a pageboy at the tender age of six. It is said that young Ibrahim had been sold to a widow who, having recognized his value, sold him to the palace. Ibrahim was put in the service of Suleyman when he was still crown prince and went with Suleyman to Manisa, where the future sultan received political training. Upon Suleyman's accession to the throne in 1520, Ibrahim became the "Has odası başı" (Master of the Privy Chamber Pages). A year later, Suleyman had a palace built for him on the hippodrome, a building that now houses the Museum of Turkish and Islamic Arts. By 1523, he became one of the youngest Grand Viziers ever and in great pomp married Suleyman's sister, Hatice, in 1524. The same year he went to Hungary on campaign as "Serdar" (Commander-in-Chief) of the army and took part in the famous Mohac battle, a place the Ottomans continued to struggle for up until the end of the sixteenth century. It was from Hungary that Ibrahim brought back three ancient bronze statues which caused a public outcry, since he had them placed in front of his palace on the hippodrome. Islam prohibits images of all kinds, most fervently three dimensional images of the human form, for it is believed they lead to idolatry. Although having amassed many titles and much prestige on his way to what looked like was going to be a brilliant career, Ibrahim had simply made too many enemies and was executed by strangulation in Topkapi Palace in 1536. While the reasons for his murder are not clear, it appears to have been a reaction to his arrogance and extravagance in diplomacy, as well as perhaps his irreligious attitude. It is often said that Hurrem, Suleyman's favorite concubine, may have influenced his downfall, but there were plenty of others who had far greater reasons for plotting his elimination. It may even be that she tried to help him, but alas, it seems that women are simply easier to blame for the downfalls of men.

Another interesting career was that of Rustem Pasha, who also entered the palace school as a pageboy together with his brother. He was born around 1500 in a village near Sarajevo in Bosnia, though some sources say his family was Croatian. His first recorded post was as "Silahdar" (Weapons Bearer) during the Mohac campaign. By 1538 he had become Governor of Anatolia, an extremely important post. The same year he became a vizier and married Mihrimah Sultan, the daughter of Suleyman and Hurrem. He was then promoted to the position of Grand Vizier in 1544, a position he held until his death in 1561, with the exception of a two year period of dismissal. He was certainly the longest serving Grand Vizier of Suleyman the Magnificent and he was especially successful at filling the coffers of the Ottoman treasury, in addition to amassing his own personal fortune. Through the sale of government offices, his policies promoted corruption which later grew to great dimensions. Rustem may have been responsible for the conspiracy against Prince Mustafa, which led to his assasination, thus opening the doors to Hurrem's sons, one of whom finally became sultan at the age of fifty-two, as Selim II. Once again, Hurrem has been blamed, but it should be pointed out that Suleyman was reigning in very good form and continued to do so at the time Mustafa was executed. In addition to being the patron of many medreses (Koranic schools), caravansarays, and imarets (soup kitchens) in Istanbul and Anatolia, Rustem Pasha will always be remembered for the mosque, considered to be a small masterpiece of Ottoman architecture and Iznik tile work, which he had the architect Sinan build in the Eminonu district of Istanbul, near the Golden Horn.

The most valuable sources to tell us about inner palace life are accounts of former royal pages. Particularly well-known among them are the accounts of Giovanni Angiolello, an Italian who was a page during the reign of Mehmed II, and Albert Bobovi, a Polish page whose memoirs have provided a wealth of information about the late seventeenth century.

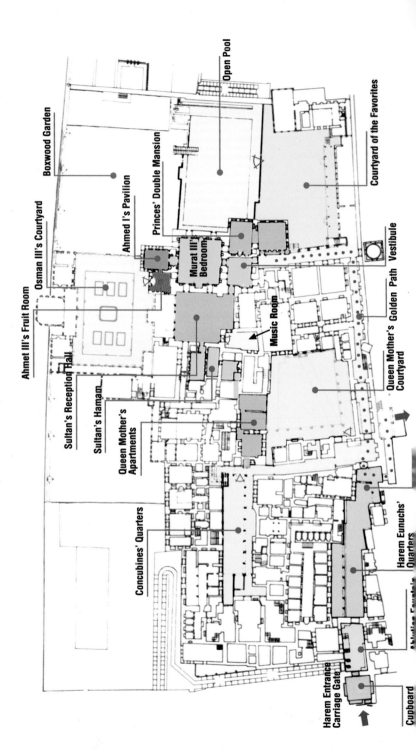

Map of the Harem section

Boxwood Garden

Open Pool

Osman III's Courtyard

Courtyard of the Favorites

Ahmet III's Fruit Room

Ahmed I's Pavilion

Princes' Double Mansion

Murat III's Bedroom

Vestibule

Sultan's Reception Hall

Music Room

Golden Path

Sultan's Hamam

Queen Mother's Apartments

Queen Mother's Courtyard

Concubines' Quarters

Harem Eunuchs' Quarters

Ablution Fountain

Harem Entrance Carriage Gate

Cupboard

# Harem

The Harem entrance is located under the shadow of the Tower of Justice in the left hand corner of the second courtyard. The area requires a separate ticket and is only accessible with a guide provided by the museum who leads visitors through a portion of the Harem for an approximately 30 minute tour. The following description follows the path of the guided tour and does not attempt to describe the entire Harem.

Harem means by definition "taboo" or "sacred." What is referred to as the "Harem section" is one part of the inner household. It is worth keeping in mind that of the over three hundred rooms of the Harem section, only four areas are certainly identified: The Sultan's quarters, the Queen Mother's quarters, the Courtyard of the Concubines (or female slaves) and the Black Eunuchs' Courtyard. The functions of many of the rooms are impossible to identify due to a lack of first hand descriptions as well as a continuous rebuilding of rooms that has made it into the labyrinth that it is today. Even the names given

Courtyard of the Favorites

to the various rooms and court-yards are later inventions based on some imaginative elaboration of

Harem Eunuchs' quarters

historical accounts that are already highly controversial themselves.

Historians do not all agree on whether Mehmed II's palace had a Harem section, but it appears very likely since his successor, Suleyman, who was the first to actually have a "favorite" live in this section, uses the term "renova-tions" when referring to the prepa-rations for receiving his "haseki," Hurrem (known as Roxelana in the West). Later, Murad III had the Harem enlarged greatly when he moved his Privy Chamber there while major renovations commis-sioned by Mehmed IV took place after a devastating fire in 1655. It seems clear that every sultan ordered some renovations and additions according to changing needs and taste.

Entering through the **Carriage Gate**, so called because when Harem ladies went on outings they exited through this gate in closed carriages, you arrive at a small domed space known as the **Domed Cupboard Room** (Dolaplı

Kubbe). Here, records of deeds were kept in the built-in cupboards of the walls for the use of the Harem eunuchs. Besides serving as guardians of the Harem, these eunuchs also controlled the finances of the Harem and of the imperial mosques of the Empire, so they often became very rich and powerful, indeed. The finances of the holy shrines of Mecca and Medina together with the imperial deeds were under their supervision until 1908.

Passing through a wide door-way, you enter the **Ablution Fountain Chamber** (Şadırvanlı Sofa). Although the fountain no longer exists, it was here that the eunuchs used to performed their ablutions before praying in the masjid, which can be reached via the door on the left, although it is rarely open today. On the left side of the room, a raised platform with steps leading up on either side served for the sultan to mount and dismount his horse before entering the Harem.

A domed entrance leads to an open courtyard that contains the **Harem eunuchs' quarters**, a two-story building on the left.

Harem Eunuchs' quarters

Seventeenth century ceramic tiles in hues of blue and green decorated with black calligraphic Arabic script in medallions cover the walls around the courtyard. The names and attributes of Allah (merciful, omniscient, forgiving, compassionate, wise, Master of the Worlds, Lord of the Day of Judgement,

Tile detail

creator, preserver, destroyer, and many more) as well as praise for the Prophet Mohammed and his companions are the subject of this script. The eunuchs lived in small tiled cubicles with grated windows, though it must not be forgotten that many of the Harem eunuchs built palaces where they later retired. If you manage to look through one of the grated windows on the left, you will observe that there is another courtyard surrounded by more dormitory rooms beyond this courtyard. Though not open to the public, rooms leading to the left after the dormitory section were apparently used as the princes' school during part of the seventeenth and eighteenth centuries, which is likely

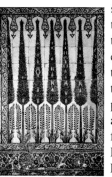

Tile detail

since one of the duties of the Harem eunuchs was to educate the young princes. The apartments for the Head Harem Eunuch as

well as those eunuchs who held other prestigious positions, such as treasurer and sultan's personal servant, are also located around this courtyard. Although it is often claimed that there was one eunuch for each room of the Harem, seeing as there are over 300 Harem rooms and it is well known that the number of eunuchs fluctuated between 70 and 100, this obviously was not the case.

At the end of the courtyard you will reach the The **Main Harem Door** (Cümle Kapısı), which separates the Harem eunuchs' quarters from the rest of the Harem. The inscription above the door reads: "Oh believers! Do not enter the Prophet's houses except when leave is given to you... And when

Main Harem Door

you ask his wives for anything, ask them from behind a screen, for that is pure for their hearts... Nor should you ever marry his wives after his death." (Surat Al-Ahzâb, verse 53) Through the Main Door, you enter a transition space known as the Guards' Place, which has a large Venetian mirror on the right. Three openings lead from this space. If you go straight ahead on the right a doorway leads to the Golden Path, a long corridor from which the visitor generally exits. In the middle is a wide gate that opens on to the courtyard known as the Courtyard of the Queen Mother (Valide Taşlığı); it is this opening that also serves as the main light source for the "Guards' Place." Finally, to the left is a small passage with marble counters for placing meals prepared in the kitchens of the second courtyard, from which one is generally lead past the "Courtyard of Concubines" to the Queen Mother's apartments.

The area known as the **Courtyard of Concubines** (Cariye Avlusu) is composed of a two-story building surrounding a narrow open courtyard with a colonnade on one side. A domed bath and what may be a kitchen are located to the left. In the Harem hierarchy, the young novice girls who resided in this section were the lowest ranking, but they were the youngest and therefore had a good chance of becoming the sultan's favorite consort. The larger building's rooms served as dormitories and study areas for girls when they first entered the Harem. They slept about ten to a room with candles constantly burning so that the elderly servants in charge could easily monitor them. They were in training, for above all else the Harem was an educational institution intended to create a

The Queen Mother's Apartments

female elite class of consorts to the sultan as well as wives for the royal pages when they took on positions outside of the palace. In addition to learning how to read and write, speak proper Ottoman Turkish, Muslim religious practices, handicrafts, and domestic skills, the Harem women were also trained in both dance and music.

The concubines' quarters surround a narrow, rather small and suffocating courtyard. In addition to the living quarters you see here, there are more concubine dormitories at the opposite end of the corridor as well. A stairway in the corner of this courtyard leads up to the Headmistresses' Apartment (Kalfalar Dairesi). The head-

Kütahya tiles

who look onto closed courtyards, not too mention spaciousness. Just as those of the sultan, the Queen Mother's rooms, too, consist of a bedroom, reception room, sitting room, and domed "hamam" (bath) that is linked with the sultan's own bath facilities via a corridor. The rooms on view here to date are the "Sitting Room" together with a small, attached room that may have been used as a bedroom and private prayer space. Most visitors find the window between the Sitting Room and the bedroom unnecessary, but it seems that the small room was built onto the sitting room at a later date and so the window once actually commanded quite a view! The raised platform on one side of the room may have been where the Queen Mother dined in private, looking out toward the Golden Horn. Kütahya tile revetments with the three-ball, double stripe pattern in hues of blue and white date from the late seventeenth century, while the neoclassical fresco paintings of figureless landscapes date to the eighteenth and nineteenth centuries.

mistresses had supervisory positions taking care of the day-to-day business of the Harem laundry and overseeing the pantry, treasury, coiffeurs, baths, coffee makers, and scribes. They received the highest stipends of all the palace servants. A hospital for the Harem women stands beyond these dormitories, but is currently not open for viewing.

A passage to the right opposite the courtyard leads to the **Queen Mother's Apartments** (Valide Dairesi). There appears to be a very obvious difference in the rank of individuals in terms of those who have a view of the outside world versus those

The taste for landscape paintings with views of wooden mansions and the sea developed in the eighteenth century. The complete absence of human figures, as in other parts of the palace, is due to their prohibition in Islamic law. A corridor leads to the

Dome

Hamam passage

which are dominated by darkness, these bath sections are bathed in the sunlight that enters from its domed ceilings.

The Hamam dressing room was for enjoying sweet coffee and music after the bath, besides dressing and undressing, while the hot room was where elderly female attendants would scrub, then massage and lather, and, finally, continuously pour bowls of water over the sultan while he sat on the warm marble seats. You can see a narrow room with a Turkish toilet and taps for washing next to it at the end of the Hamam. Being located almost exactly in the center of the

Toilet

Queen Mother's bath, which is a smaller version of that of the sultan.

In the **Sultan's Hamam**, as in any other Turkish bath, the order of rooms is: dressing room, cool room, and hot room. The white walls of the bath and the white marble basins with their newly gilt taps contrast strikingly with the colorful tiles of the other rooms. The rooms of the bath must have originally been revetted with tiles, one panel of which was reset on the "Golden Path," which you will see as you exit. Unlike the small rooms of the living areas,

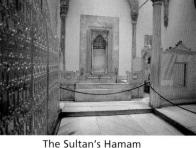

The Sultan's Hamam

Harem area, this double hamam that served the sultan on one side and his mother on the other, also provides a transition area between male and female space.

The grand room that follows the Sultan's Hamam is the **Royal Reception Hall** (Hünkâr Sofası), the largest single room in the Harem. It functioned primarily as a place where the sultan would sit on his throne while the Queen Mother and other female members of the family as well as favorites would gather under the arcade

Bath slippers

Basin

Royal Reception Hall

on the long divans to enjoy entertainment, usually performed by
female dancers, musicians, or
acrobats. The hall very likely
dates to Mehmed IV's
rebuilding of the Harem
after the 1655 fire, including
the dome, measuring nearly
eleven meters in diameter.
More visible, however, is
the grand rococo style reno-
vation work carried out by
order of Osman III in the
mid-eighteenth century. A
raised arcaded platform in

Fountain

heavy rococo style was added on
the side with the windows, where
most of the light comes in, to
accommodate blindfolded male
musicians. You can peak into a
small music room with a gilt piano
from France and some Turkish
musical instruments, like the ud
and ney flute you see on the
couch, located on the right side of
the hall. The eighteenth century
blue and white Delft tiles from

Holland that cover the walls some-
how seem out of place, but by then
the Iznik and Kütahya factories
had stopped producing quality
tiles, so the sultans turned
to Europe to import new
ones. The huge Chinese
vases, Queen Victoria's gift
of the twin standing English
clocks with Arabic numerals
(which are set at five past
nine, the time Mustafa
Kemal Atatürk, father of the
Turkish Republic, died in
Dolmabahçe Palace on
November 11, 1938), and the
fountains presented by Wilhelm II
of Germany on dis-
play here give this
room an eclectic
appearance. As in
other parts of the
palace, Italian stained
glass windows add
color and light while a
giant Bohemian crys-
tal chandelier hangs in

Delft tiles

Sultan Murad III's Bedroom

fireplace on the north wall faces a tiered built-in marble fountain or "selsebil." The sound of flowing water is considered one of the sounds of paradise in Islam, so fountains are often found inside palaces as well as in courtyards. It is said that it was also a way by which the sultan could have secret conversations, since there were many ears in the palace and the flowing water masked low voices. Although Sultan Murad III may have slept in this room at times, it is difficult to say, as a sultan slept wherever he felt tired. Mattresses were rolled out for him whereever he decided to sleep and attendants were on duty to watch over him all night long, unless dismissed. Likewise, traditional Turkish homes generally do not designate one room for sleeping. While his attendants in the Harem section would be female, it was male

the center of the room.

From the Reception Hall, you pass to a vestibule, the walls of which are covered by exquisite Iznik tiles. Tiles of the same type are also found in the great domed room known as **Murad III's Bedroom**, into which this vestibule leads. This great domed pavilion is the only sixteenth century structure in the Harem in which original tile decorations have been preserved. The structure might be

Dome

the work of the architect, Sinan, who was commissioned by Murad III to build the sultan's private rooms in the Harem. The room occupies a perfect square and the dome supported by pendentives is 10.30 meters in diameter. The colors of the tiles are various shades of blue and green with some red. The red is slightly raised and if you touch the tiles, you can feel the difference in surface level. The red is called "Armenian bole," a thick slip with a high iron oxide content to produce the deep orangey-red color. The gilt bronze

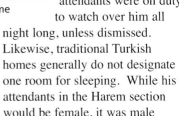

Tiered marble fountain

Sultan Ahmed I's Pavilion

pageboys who performed this duty outside of the Harem area. Knowing that Murad III fathered 103 children by almost as many concubines, one cannot help but wonder whether some of these amorous encounters took place in the aforementioned "bedroom." A gold pendant hangs down from the center of the dome of the bedroom reminding us that we are in an imperial hall. The inscription in a continuous band of blue and white tile around the whole room is the throne verse from the Koran, according to tradition the holiest verse of the holiest Surat Al-Baqara (the Cow). It reads: "Allah! None has the right to be worshipped but Allah, the Ever living, the All-sustaining and All protecting... His throne extends over the heavens and the earth..." (2:255) This verse is found in several of the palace rooms, most importantly the Throne Room of the previous Privy Chamber where the holy relics are now kept and in the Baghdad Pavilion.

Subsequent additions have obstructed Murad III's Bedroom's earlier view of the Golden Horn and a marble courtyard that is also a later addition has yet to be open to visitors. A small room was added to the large domed "bedroom" by Murad III's grandson, Ahmed I. This room, known as **Ahmed I's Pavilion**, would have allowed the sultan and his visitors to gaze upon the Golden Horn and may have been used for private prayer,

Niche

as indicated by the blue and white floral tiles recalling the Blue Mosque. The triangular pendentives of the dome are covered with a green tile with verses written in calligraphic script. Producing such tiles is extremely difficult since they must curve slightly to fit the form of the pendentive.

A century later, Ahmed III added another small room,

Iznik tiles

Sultan Ahmed III's "Fruit Room"

the edge of the courtyard, notably Selim III's "Music Room" and the bedroom where Abdulhamid I slept in the late eighteenth century.

At this point you are led back through the sultan's bedroom and vestibule to the **Princes' Double Mansion** (Şehzadeler Çift Kasırlar). Serving to further obstruct the original view and light source of Murat III's Bedroom, these rooms were built on the south wall sometime in the early seventeenth century. The two rooms are each a perfect square, covered with floral green, blue, red, and white Iznik tiles. Each room has a fireplace, both of which were originally gilt in bronze, although one of them is now plaster. Colorful stained-glass windows glitter like mosaics when the sun comes in. The first room the visitor enters is domed and is one of the few original inlaid wooden domes of the palace. There was a pendant hanging from this dome, indicating

called **Fruit Room** (Yemiş Odası), next to that of Ahmed I. Decorated with delicately painted colorful fruits and flowers together with a frieze of Arabic and Persian poetry in gold calligraphic script that encircles it, the room is said to have functioned as a space for the sultan to have his meals in privacy. More likely, it allowed this sultan, who so loved his flower gardens in the spring and summer, to gaze in the winter months upon the flowers and fruits on the walls as he indulged himself in reading poetry, which was a favorite pastime of his. Looking out the windows from the Fruit Room, you can catch a glimpse of a white marble court with a pond and a pavilion, all of which was built by Osman III in the mid-eighteenth century. Although not open to visitors, many more rooms and pavilions continue around

Princes' Double Mansion

Dome

that it was a sultan's room. Often erroneously translated as "Crown Prince," "Şehzade" is in fact a title given to all sons of the sultan, so these rooms may have been used by princes at some later period, hence the name. However, like so many of the rooms of the Harem, their function is far from certain.

Courtyard of the Favorites

From the double mansion, you exit to a large open courtyard called the **Paved Courtyard of the Favorites** (Gözdeler Taşlığı)

Open Pool (left)

which, in addition to acting as a terrace overlooking a pool, commands a fantastic view of the Golden Horn. When you look out from this terrace, to the left you can see the huge arches upon which the Murad III's Bedroom's pavilion and vestibule rest, while further north to the left, more arches support the marble courtyard and pond that the Fruit Room looks upon. Underneath Murad III's bedroom, there is a fountain together with large basins perhaps used as a cool retreat on hot summer days. The courtyard below

has been called the Elephant Garden (Fil Bahçesi) and also **Boxwood Garden** (Şimşirlik), though what you see today is neither elephants nor boxwood trees, but an area covered primarily by a large shallow pond. The names, of course, imply, however, that we may very well have seen elephants and/or boxwoods here in the time of the sultans. In fact, the foundations of a pavilion called "The Elephant House" have been located in the courtyard and may have housed one of the elephants brought from India for the sultan's delight. While boxwood is a native bush, found commonly in gardens as a hedging plant, it was also prized in woodworking for its hard close-grained yellow wood, so it is possible that something made of boxwood, rather than the hedge bush itself, may have given it this particular name.

The white two-story structures made of wood and stone looking directly onto the Courtyard of the

Open Pool (right)

Courtyard of the Favorites

Favorites are late eighteenth century buildings in the Ottoman house style; at the moment the interior is not open to visitors. The overhanging bay windows are designed for built-in divans and built specifically for enjoying the view. Although the name implies a connection with the women who were "gözde," as a concubine who had caught the sultan's eye was called, concubines did not reside in this section of the Harem until perhaps the end of the eighteenth century, if at all. It appears that Abdulhamid I commissioned at least a section of the building at the east end corner where a "Mabeyn" for entertainment, also known as the "Mirrored Room," is located. This particular sultan, who at the age of forty-nine ascended to the throne to reign for fourteen years until his death in 1789, spent most of his life sequestered in the Harem by his sultan brother. Referred to as "The Cage," the place where he lived during his sequester was located at the western corner of this courtyard. Despite its name, there was never actually a cage or prison of any sort here; rather, "The Cage" is indicative of the place where the sultan's brother would be carefully guarded within the Harem. In fact, the "caged" brothers of sultans would ride a horse every week to the Friday prayer in Haghia Sophia, the imperial mosque, as well as have teachers come in to educate them. Treatment of such brothers –as well as sons and nephews when they were deemed a threat–, however, varied according to sultan. It should be noted that, despite living in the Harem section, none of the captive males had access to the concubines.

The love letters written by Abdulhamid I reveal a romantic side of this sultan who, although the limit was normally four, went

*Terrace of the Serraglio* by J.L. Gerome

so far as to have eleven favorite women at one time! Perhaps the Mabeyn was for entertaining his favorites. It seems clear that he was used to staying in the Harem and even preferred it to the outside world, yet he made it a point to get to know the city as well. He ordered the construction of public fountains,

*Beethoven in the Harem* by Abdul Mecid Efendi

Koranic schools, a large mosque in Beylerbeyi, and a large market complex near the Golden Horn. While fires devastated many parts of the city and left thousands homeless, the Ottoman Empire's war with Russia and Austria wrought havoc upon the people. It was perhaps these particulr circumstances of the time that led Abdulhamid I to have his nephew, the future Sultan Selim III, educated and prepared for his role as sultan rather than sequestering him. And indeed, certainly in part due to his uncle's foresight, Selim III was to become one of the most enlightened sultans the Ottoman line ever produced.

A last point should be made regarding the Harem. Many imperial pavilions built along the shores of the promontory of the

*Odalisque and Slave* by J.A.D. Ingres

Topkapi grounds, as well as along the Golden Horn and the Bosphorus, during the seventeenth and eighteenth centuries were later destroyed by fires or torn down for building roads and railways. These magnificent pavilions are known through sketches, paintings, and in some cases photographs. While these pavilions served as spring and summer residences of the sultan and other members of his household, the Topkapi Harem was used during the winter, hence the small rooms that were much easier to heat during the cold months, although it is also true that some sultans rarely spent a night in Topkapi Palace.

Tile detail

and offer a gold coin to the girl that he had chosen for that night. More likely, however, the name is connected to this being the sultan's primary walkway. The path leads back toward the entrance to the Main Harem Door (Cümle Kapısı), where you will turn left to exit into the third courtyard next to the **Aviary** (Kuşhane) just behind the mosque.

As you conclude your visit to the Harem, you will walk through a passage known as the **Golden Path** (Altın Yol). Popular stories attribute its name to the practice of a sultan who would walk along the path lined with girls on either side

Harem exit

## QUESTIONS

32. Using 19th century depictions of Harem life, what is the general impression of the Harem expressed by each artist? How do they differ, how are they similar?

    Jean Leon Gerome, *Terrace of the Seraglio*, 1842 (p. 84, bottom)
    Abdul Mecid Efendi, *Beethoven in the Harem*, 1875 (p. 85, top)
    Jean Auguste Dominique Ingres, *Odalisque and Slave*, 1832 (p. 85, bottom)

# Women of the Imperial Harem

Few places have inspired so much fantasizing by so many people as the Imperial Harem. To get at the truth about this curious place that continues to fascinate –thanks in part to much tale-spinning– one must sift through many highly imaginative descriptions and depictions, as I have tried to do here for this brief exposè on the women who occupied this particular corner of Topkapi.

Until Suleyman the Magnificent's favorite, Hurrem, moved into the Harem, Valide Sultans (Queen Mothers), concubines, princes, and princesses lived in the "Old Palace," which is the first palace built by Mehmed II. Evidence indicates that a Harem or female area was most likely part of the original palace construction and that it began as a very small area that eventually reached large dimensions by the end of the seventeenth century.

The Imperial Harem served as a training institution for future concubines of the sultan and wives of the elite royal pages as well as a residential area. Young girls were spotted in the slave markets of the empire and, if they were particularly beautiful or talented, they were presented to a vizier or the head eunuch. Greek, Italian, French, Ukrainian, and Circassian were among the most prized women.

Almost every sultan's mother was of Christian origin. Upon entrance, they converted to Islam and were given new names. The young novices lived in dormitories much like the royal pages. According to one late-sixteenth century description by Queen Elizabeth I's organist, Thomas Dallam, with their baggy trousers and tunics, their attire was much like that of the pages as well, only the girls' trousers were brightly colored and translucent, showing their fair ankles. Dalam describes the girls playing in the Boxwood Garden in colorful, diaphanous shalvar pants and short tunics with their long hair braided. However, this oft-cited account is dubious as it is highly unlikely that he would have been able to see any of the females of the Harem. In addition, the Shakespearian prose in which his account is written also casts doubt upon its authenticity, it being unlikey that an organist would have such a fine command of language.

The training of the girls was rigorous and they had very little free time for lounging about in the baths, as many Westerners have fantasized. Their teachers were the older expert women who had entered the Harem as slaves, like them, until the mid-sixteenth century when their mentor became the Queen Mother herself. They all learned to read, write, and speak Ottoman Turkish properly. Embroidery was a specialty of the Harem and they often sold their work through Jewish tradeswomen. Many of the girls became expert singers, musicians, and seamstresses. Usually by the age of sixteen or seventeen, they were married to royal pages or other men of high rank with an abundant dowry and, of course, manumitted.

There was a rule of silence and so mutes were included in the Harem to teach sign language. Mute women were generally hairdressers in the Harem and earned a good salary. All of the women of the Harem earned a daily stipend depending on their positions, records of which were kept and can be inspected today. While the mother of a sultan was by far the highest ranking woman of the Harem, the various headmistresses known as "kalfa"s had the job of supervising the many everyday tasks in the Harem, for example the pantry, the treasury, laundry, and baths, for which they were all handsomely paid. Those women of the Harem who bore children of the sultan or rose to high ranks of service would move to larger private rooms and with age retire to the Old Palace. Opon the accession of a new sultan, most of the former sultan's Harem moved to the Old Palace; some were married off to members of the elite while a few young ones might stay on. The population of the Harem varied greatly; in 1574 (Selim II): 49, in 1600 (Mehmed III): 275, in 1652 (Mehmed IV): 436.

"Valide Sultan" (Queen Mother) is a title that was given to the mother of the reigning sultan. This title first appears in the late-sixteenth century to refer to Nurbanu, mother of Murat III. However, the first woman to act like a

Valide Sultan, albeit sans the title, was Suleyman the Magnificent's favorite, Hurrem.

Rigorously in favor of her sons and wielding great influence over the sultan, Hurrem is popularly known in the West as Roxelana. Although she herself did not live to become a Valide, one of her sons did become sultan: Selim II, whose favorite Nurbanu was to be the first titular Valide. The period between 1566 and 1656 is known as the "Age of the Queen Mother" or the "Sultanate of Women" because of the influence these women had upon the sultan. They played important roles in the private affairs of the sultan, ensuring that an heir would be produced, and, in case of the sultan's death, that an heir would be on hand to take over immediately. They also played a role in the official affairs of the empire, taking over when the sultan was either too young or incompetent, or even complementing the sultan in his correspondence with foreign powers to create and maintain alliances. Nurbanu, mother of Murat III, corresponded with the French dowager queen, Catherine de Medicis, while Safiye, mother of Mehmed III exchanged letters with Queen Elizabeth of England. Another important Valide Sultan, Kosem, mother of two sultans, Murad IV and "Crazy" Ibrahim is said to have saved the Ottoman dynasty from extinction by saving Ibrahim from being killed by his brother the sultan Murad IV, who died childless, and then convincing Ibrahim to procreate. The Valides' power, however, waned by the late-seventeenth century due to more Sultans reaching the throne at a mature age.

Between the mid-sixteenth century, when the sultan's favorite concubine began living in Topkapi, up until the seventeenth century, the sultan's sons stayed in the Harem with their mothers until they reached a certain age, usually around ten, at which time they would be moved together with their mothers to provincial capitals where they would receive political training. When their fathers died, the princes would race to Istanbul to seize the throne and have their brothers executed. This practice ceased, however, in the seventeenth century when, rather than executing their brothers, the sultans began holding them hostage.

"Haseki" is a title given to the sultan's favorite concubine. Suleyman the Magnificent was particularly devoted to his haseki, Hurrem. She was the first to move into the Harem section of the palace and she lived close to the sultan until her death in 1558. Although she had commissioned a large pious foundation with a mausoleum for herself to be built, Suleyman preferred for her to be buried with him in his "türbe" (tomb) behind his own mosque complex, the Suleymaniye. "Valide"s generally started as "haseki"s. "Gözde" or "in the eye" of the sultan is another title used to refer to the sultan's favorite.

"Ikbal" was used to refer to a woman who had been singled out to become a "kadın" (concubine) of the sultan and therefore lived in larger quarters than the "cariye" (servant). The servants slept six to eight to a room while the concubines were in rooms of four or five. A concubine who produced a child was given private quarters and if the child was a girl, she could raise her. The cariye were the lowest ranking, and generally the youngest of the Harem women, and they lived in dormitories performing menial tasks, but also studying Turkish, Islam, embroidery, music, etc. "Odalık," translated as "odalisque," but literally meaning chambermaid, is another term designating servant as well.

After 1800, almost all of the women who entered the sultan's Harem were Circassians, and hence Muslims. Although Islam forbids the buying and selling of Muslims, apparently a loophole made this practice, considered a pre-Islamic Circassian tradition, acceptable in that the existence of a slave class in Circassian society was used as justification to override the ban on Muslim slaves and thereby recruit its girls and women into harems. Besides, Circassians were often considered Muslims in name only. The fair-skinned, blue-eyed girls were valued for their physical traits. Circassians fled the Russian advance in Crimea and the Caucasus, escaping into Ottoman territories on the Black Sea in the late-eigteenth and early-nineteenth centuries. This incident coincided with the flood of Circassian girls into the Imperial Harem.

With the "Young Turk" revolution of 1908, Sultan Abdulhamid II was forced to leave Istanbul and manumit the Harem girls and eunuchs. By then, the majority of the girls were Circassian and so their parents or relatives came to fetch them. However, some were never taken back to their homes and ended up as a stageshow traveling in Europe. It was a time when women in the Ottoman Empire were just getting a taste of freedom and wealthy educated families stopped the male-female division in their own homes.

# Eunuchs

Eunuchs were boys taken into slavery and castrated, generally before puberty. They were primarily in charge of guarding the Harem and the inner section of the palace, though they also instructed young princes and pageboys. Although Islam forbids castration viruently, eunuchs were bought and sold in Muslim territories until the beginning of the twentieth century, especially for the purpose of guarding and protecting the harems of wealthy men. The white eunuchs were generally boys from the Christian populations of the Balkans sold into slavery through piracy or poverty, while the black eunuchs came from the non-Muslim populations of East Africa. A eunuch was worth twice as much as a non-castrated boy in the slave markets of Istanbul or Cairo.

The Ottoman tradition of employing chief eunuchs as guards dates to Murat II, 1421-51, who probably borrowed the custom from the Seljuk kingdoms of Rum and they from earlier Islamic kingdoms. The Byzantines also employed eunuchs, especially in the army. Mehmet II appears to be the first sultan to employ African eunuchs and until the end of the sixteenth century, black and white eunuchs worked and lived side by side. In 1582, the superintendence of the Harem passed to the black eunuchs and they held the most important positions since it was at that time that the power of the empire was often in the hands of the Queen Mother, with the chief black eunuch as her closest emissary to the outside world. The black eunuchs also administered all of the finances of imperial pious foundations in Istanbul, which included mosques, soup kitchens for the poor, Koranic schools, baths, etc., as well as the pious foundations in the holy cities of Mecca and Medina. Upon retirement, the eunuchs generally took their great wealth and settled in Mecca; however, upon their death, all of their money and possessions returned to the sultan.

Chief eunuchs carried the title "Aga" or "Master," as in "Master of the Gate" or "Harem Master," and it was the sultan who assigned them directly to their positions. There are many famous eunuchs who reached important levels within the Ottoman government. Gazanfer Ağa, who together with his brother had been sold on the slave market as a young boy by pirates because his widowed mother did not have enough money to pay for his ransom, became Master of the Gate. His is an unusual story because he and his brother entered the palace as royal pages at first, then realizing that the most powerful person was the Master of the Gate, after puberty they both decided to become eunuchs and so had themselves castrated. His brother did not survive the operation, but Gazanfer became Master of the Gate and his wealth so great that he had his mother and sisters come from Italy to live in great mansions while his brother-in-law was granted trading privileges. He also commissioned a medrese complex, or Koranic school where he was buried in 1596; the same building today houses the Museum of Caricature and Humor.

Hacı Beşir Ağa was an African eunuch who entered the palace as a young boy to then go on to become Master of the Harem at a very young age. He held his position through the reigns of both Ahmet III and Mahmud I (1703-1745), though he was exiled to Cyprus for a short time by the Grand Vizier in an attempt to curb his power. With his great wealth, he built schools, mosques, and libraries in many cities of the Empire: Istanbul, Baghdad, Cairo, Medina, Mecca, and Bursa. Without Beşir's approval, the sultan would not assign important positions. He was also an astute diplomat in directing relations between Iran and the Ottoman Empire. He died in 1746 at the age of 94, so they say, but no one ever wrote down the birthdate of an African eunuch, so this number is far from certain. His tomb is located near the Mosque of Eyyub, in a prestigious cemetary for the pious.

In 1715, the grand vizier Shehid Ali Pasha tried to abolish the castration of Africans, although not for humanitarian reasons, but rather to put a cap on their influence over the sultan. In the end, he was unsuccessful. Even after Mahmud II passed an edict to abolish the slave trade and castration, it persisted, especially in the palace. By the mid-nineteenth century, the eunuchs' main occupation was to watch over the Harem women, deciding whether their dress was appropriate and allowing or refusing visitors. Over time, Harem eunuchs lost their place in the government and society.

The sexual feelings and parts of eunuchs have been the subject of almost as much fantasizing as that of the Harem concubines. Though there might have been some amorous sentiment between a eunuch and a Harem woman, it would be completely out of place for a eunuch to break the barrier and his life would have been taken in an instant, as would that of the woman. With a chance to become the concubine of a sultan one day, why risk an affair with a eunuch slave?  It seems more likely that a eunuch might fall in love with a woman outside the Harem, but then how would he ever be able to meet her considering the divisions between males and females in Ottoman society?  Besides, a boy who is castrated grows up into an odd looking man with a high voice whose condition would be obvious to a woman of the time.  It has been said that the castration of African eunuchs was complete while the European eunuchs had only their testicles removed, and not the penis, thus rendering the African more precious for guarding the Harem. Although there is no way to ascertain the truth of this, it could be accurate.

# Brief Chronology Of The Ottoman Empire

- **1290?-1320?:** Osman, for whom the Ottoman dynasty is named, begins conquest in Anatolia.
- **1326:** Sultan Orhan, son of Osman, establishes first Ottoman capital in Bursa.
- **1371-1375:** Sultan Murad I, son of Orhan, invades Serbia.
- **1389:** Sultan Murad I dies in the Battle of Kosovo.
- **1394:** Sultan Bayezid I, son of Murad, occupies Bulgaria.
- **1402:** Tamerlane from the East defeats and captures Sultan Bayezid I in Ankara.
- **1413:** Sultan Mehmed I, son of Beyazid I, becomes sultan after a long struggle with his brothers.
- **1421:** Sultan Murad II, son of Mehmed I, establishes a new Ottoman capital in Edirne (Adrianopolis).
- **1451:** Sultan Murad II abdicates in favor of his son, Mehmed II.
- **1453:** Sultan Mehmed II, "The Conqueror," takes Constantinople on May 29th and establishes new capital of the Ottoman Empire there.
- **1461-1474:** Sultan Mehmed II takes the Empire of Trabzon, the Karaman region of central Anatolia, Bosnia, and Crimea.
- **1478:** Topkapi Palace is completed as the sultan's residence and administrative center.
- **1485-1491:** Sultan Bayezid II at war with Mamluks in Egypt and Syria.
- **1489:** First violent earthquake after Ottoman conquest in Istanbul.
- **1514:** Sultan Selim I is victorious against Safavids in Iran.
- **1517:** Sultan Selim I conquers Mamluk Syria and Egypt, then occupies Algeria.
- **1522-1534:** Suleyman "The Magnificent" conquers Rhodes, invades Hungary, attacks Vienna, and takes Baghdad.
- **1528:** Hurrem (Roxelana), Sultan Suleyman's favorite, moves into the Harem section of Topkapi Palace, thereby beginning a new tradition.
- **1557:** Violent earthquake in Istanbul.
- **1571:** Sultan Selim II occupies Cyprus.
- **1571:** Ottomans are defeated at tha Battle Of Lepanto.
- **1574:** Sultan Murad III moves Privy Chamber into the Harem section of Topkapi.
- **1595:** Safiye Valide, mother of Sultan Mehmed III, moves into the Harem to be near her son, setting a new tradition.
- **1648:** Major earthquake in Istanbul.
- **1655:** Fire devastates Harem and Sultan Mehmed IV orders rebuilding.
- **1669:** Turkish Embassy sent to France.

- **1703-1720:** "Tulip Period" coinciding with Sultan Ahmet III's reign; European influences first felt.
- **1768-1774:** Ottomans at war with Russians under Catherine the Great.
- **1763:** Earthquake damages Topkapi and Sultan Mustafa III orders restoration.
- **1787-1792:** Ottomans at war with Russia and Austria.
- **1783:** Russians annex the Crimean Peninsula.
- **1793:** Sultan Selim III proclaims the "New Order" troops with European style uniforms and formations.
- **1798-1802:** French Expedition to Egypt
- **1803:** Wahhabites of Saudi Arabia occupy the Holy Cities of Mecca and Medina.
- **1803:** Begining Of Ali Pasha of Ioannina's revolt against Ottoman authority in Northern Greece.
- **1803:** Begining of Serbian insurrection against Ottomans.
- **1812:** Governor Mehmed Ali's revolt against Ottoman authority in Egypt begins.
- **1812:** Terrible outbreak of plague in Istanbul empties the city.
- **1829:** Greek Independence.
- **1839:** British take Aden on the Red Sea.
- **1839:** Sultan Mahmud II orders Proclamation Of Rights in Gülhane Park.
- **1856:** Sultan Abdul Mecid moves to newly completed Dolmabahçe Palace, after which Topkapi ceases to be the sultan's official residence.
- **1861-1878:** Sultan Abdul Aziz orders many of the shore pavilions around Topkapi to be torn down to make way for schools, military barracks, and the railway.
- **1878:** Independence of Serbia, Romania, and Bulgaria. Austrians take Bosnia and Herzegovina, Russians occupy eastern Anatolia.
- **1908:** Young Turk Revolution, Sultan Abdul Hamid II is forced to flee.
- **1912-1913:** Wars in the Balkans.
- **1914:** Ottoman alliance with Germany against France, England and Russia: First World War.
- **1914:** Russian invasion of eastern Anatolia.
- **1915:** Massacres and deportation of Armenians.
- **1916:** Arab revolts against Ottoman authority.
- **1917:** British take Baghdad.
- **1918:** The last Ottoman sultan, Mehmed VI, is enthroned at the Gate of Felicity in Topkapi Palace.
- **1919:** Greeks invade from Izmir.
- **1920:** War Of Independence begins.
- **1923:** Proclamation of the Turkish Republic with Mustafa Kemal as first President and Ankara as the new capital; sultanate is abolished; end of the Ottoman Empire.
- **1924:** Abdulmecid Efendi, last heir to the Ottoman throne, abdicates as last caliph.

# Answers

**1-** The Ottoman Sultan Mehmed II is called "the Conqueror" because he conquered Byzantine Constantinople in 1453 at the age of 21. Though many subsequent sultans conquered vast territories, none was given the epithet "The Conqueror" for the taking of Constantinople was a great victory and Ottoman control of Asia Minor and the Balkans would have been unlikely without hegemony over the city spanning two continents.

**2-** The location of Topkapi Palace is important because: a) it looks over three bodies of water: the Sea of Marmara, The Golden Horn and the Bosphorus Straits; b) it is on the crest of a promontory which makes it tower above the city; c) its entrance is just behind the Great Church of Haghia Sophia, symbol of Christendom in the East for 900 years until converted into a Mosque by Mehmet II; d) with only one land wall, it is secluded from the city and a safe haven for the sultan.

**3-** The portrait by the Italian painter Gentile Bellini is an almost life-size oil painting, shown on page 13 of this book. Mehmed looks to the right under a richly decorated classic gilt marble arch and a jeweled tapestry is draped over the edge in the style of Venetian painters. The Turkish (or Persian) artist shows Mehmed seated in a cross legged position wearing a brilliant blue caftan, holding a rose in his right hand which he is smelling and in his left hand a kerchief, as seen on page 12. This miniature portrait is a watercolor by Sinan Bey or Siblizade Ahmet.

**4-** Mehmed II saw himself as a world ruler and believed that his dynasty would endure forever. Previous sultans and Islamic rulers used similar words to describe themselves.

**5-** The two towers at either side of the Imperial Gate are square. There are seven towers between the Imperial Gate and the Processions Pavilion.

**6-** The high crenellated wall makes it look like a fortress. The miniature shows the original second storey, which does not exist today.

**7-** Sultan Mahmud II had the Processions Pavilion shortened so he could see and hear the rebels better.

**8-** The Imperial Gate looks more like a building built over fortress walls (especially when it had two storeys) while the Middle Gate with its high turreted towers on either side is more fanciful and impressive to the visitor.

**9-** The hospital for pages was located in the first courtyard close to the Imperial Gate presumably to keep any contagions as far away as possible from the sultan's private quarters.

**10-** White flour bread was for the sultan and his mother, although on occasion it was given to the Grand Vizier and his immediate family members as well; everyone else ate the dark coarse bread.

**11-** Straw mats were especially useful for protection from the humidity of the stone floors. They were put under carpets in the winter and simply covered the floors of summer pavilions.

12- The Imperial Gate is at the forefront of the miniature (4) while the Middle Gate is at the top. An African eunuch guards the pageboys' hospital that no longer exists and he can be seen seated between two pages. On the right is a large structure depicting Haghia Irene which was used as an armory, and a small polygonal building at the top right was a pavilion, no longer standing, for petitioners to leave their complaints that no longer stands.

13- The transition from wall to dome is made with a "muqarnas" technique; this looks something like stalactites.

14- The roof of the Tiled Pavilion is perfectly flat except for a small dome in the center and four chimneys rising up around it.

15- The conditions for entering the middle gate were to be on official business, unarmed, on foot, and silent.

16- The sultans' horses were richly "dressed" with jeweled bridles and saddles, gold and silver stirrups and frontals, etc... Hence a treasury was needed to keep these precious caparisons.

17- In the painting by Vanmour, you can see the grate of the sultan's window just above the center of the wall; the grand vizier is seated directly below it and more viziers (ministers) with their tall cylindrical hats are participating in the banquet. The French Embassy members are recognizable by their triangular hats.

18- Probably more for symbolic reasons than structural since the Tower of Justice reminded the people of their "just" ruler and it became even more visible with the heightening.

19- The kitchen chimneys, easily seen from the Sea of Marmara, are an important symbol of the sultan's benevolence since his people should never go hungry and food to be given to the populace often came from these kitchens.

20- Spices and silk were other items from China and India that came across central Asia by caravan.

21- In the miniature you can see Sultan Suleyman at the table with two guests on the right and servant boys bringing in another covered dish on the left. The table is low and round, dishes with perhaps rice pilaf have been uncovered, and small round loaves of bread together with long handled spoons are on the table.

22- Structurally, it is almost identical. In the background, Sultan Selim III is seated on his throne just under the pendant of the Gate of Felicity, surrounded by black and white eunuchs, religious authorities, and royal pages on either side. In the foreground, you can see janissaries with their fanned head gear and red-sleeved hats, while turbaned judges and the viziers with their cylindrical hats pay their respects to the sultan.

23- The portrait of Sultan Selim II is a miniature while that of Sultan Abdul Hamid I is life-size. Selim is seated cross-legged, gazing to the left with one fist on his knee and the other hand delicately poised while Abdul Hamid seems to be kneeling or cross-legged, facing the viewer directly with both hands on his knees; one holds a "tespih" or Islamic rosary.

24- Keeping the holy relics nearby was often considered protective against disease, defeat, corruption, or anything else negative.

**25-** It is called the "Spoonmaker's Diamond" because it was sold for two spoons or because the tear-drop diamond is shaped like the bowl of a spoon.

**26-** Looking at the Treasury section from the outside, you can see the two large domes of the Turkish bath on the right.

**27-** The side facing the Sea of Marmara is more richly decorated.

**28-** The marble terrace or courtyard was for pleasurable activities, such as listening to music and playing in the pool. As the name implies, the iftar canopy was for breaking the fast during the month of Ramadan, at which time food might be served to favorite household members.

**29-** You can see at least three different floral designs, maybe more!

**30-** Both the Baghdad and Erivan Pavilions are more colorful inside and out with the tiles on one and the opus sectile of the other; they are polygonal and domed with wide awnings while the Mecidiye Pavilion is a rectangle, and has rich sculptural decorations. They all command beautiful views.

**31-** Conquest provided booty and money for a sultan. The booty often included building material like tiles and marbles or even artisans who were forced to work for the sultan. Victories were usually celebrated by building a mosque or pavilions as with the Baghdad and Erivan kiosks.

**32-** The ultimate Orientalist painter, Ingres, never came to Istanbul! Ingres was a skillful painter and especially a great portraitist, but his Harem girls are almost always the same archetypical beauty. During his extensive travels in the Middle East, Gerome took photographs which he used to create the perfect architectural background of his engraving of the Marble Terrace. The partially nude women lounging around the pool is fantasy. The other painter, Abdulmecid Efendi, was the son of Sultan Abdul Aziz. He was born in 1876 and remained in the Harem by force until 1908 so his depictions of Harem life are certainly far truer to reality than those of either Ingres or Gerome, both of whom, in their own way, fed the orientalist fantasy of erotic harems. Abdulmecid was the last heir to the sultanate, though he never became sultan, serving as caliph for two years before the caliphate was abolished in 1924.

# Glossary

**ABBASID:** dynasty of caliphs (750-1258) that takes its name from the Prophet Mohammed's uncle, al-Abbas. They moved their capital to Baghdad.

**AĞA:** literally "chief" or "master". A title given to a chief eunuch in the palace or chief officer of a military squadron.

**BAYRAM:** Islamic religious feast day, the most important are the Day of Sacrifice, in celebration of the sacrifice of Abraham, and the holiday of Ramadan.

**CAFTAN:** generic term used to describe outer garment, which could be either short like a shirt or an ankle-length robe, worn with baggy shalvar pants.

**DEVSHIRME:** the system by which the Ottoman government used to levy Christian youths to be trained for posts in the palace, the administration, or the military corps.

**DIVAN:** the council or Ottoman governing organ.

**FATIH:** literally "conqueror" and epithet for Mehmet II.

**HAFIZ:** title given to an individual who has committed the Holy Koran to memory, also a reader of the Koran, the poetic form of which lends itself to chanting.

**HAREM:** literally "taboo" or "sanctuary", used to designate the area occupied by female household members and into which unrelated males were not allowed entrance.

**HASEKI:** favorite concubine of the sultan.

**IFTAR:** During the month of Ramadan, the fast is broken just after sunset with a meal called "iftar".

**IKBAL:** Woman singled out as a possible favorite companion of the sultan.

**JANISSARY:** from the Turkish "yeniçeri" meaning new troops, the sultans standing infantry corps recruited through the devshirme system.

**KADIN:** means woman in Turkish, but is a title given to, at most four, of the sultan's female favorite companions. Equivalent to "wife".

**KHAN:** Persian word for king, sultan, or leader used as a title for the Ottoman sultans.

**KIOSK:** Turkish architectural term for a garden pavilion, usually with views in all directions.

**KUL:** means slave, but was an honorable title for the slaves of the sultan.

**MAMELUK:** ruling dynasty in Egypt from 1250 to 1517, in origin slaves who made up the military class.

**MASJID:** small mosque, or prayer hall, where the Friday prayer is not led.

**MINARET:** generally a high platform, or in Ottoman architecture, a lofty, slender tower from which the prayer is called, five times daily according to Islamic principles.

**ODALISQUE:** from the Turkish "odalık" to designate a female chamber attendant or concubine.

**OTTOMAN:** from the name Osman, the putative founder of the Turkish dynasty ruling parts of Asia Minor from around 1300 eventually to rule vast territories from the Balkans to Syria and Egypt until 1922, with the disintegration of the Ottoman Empire. Refers to the old language spoken by the ruling elite which is grammaticallyTurkish but with many Persian and Arabic words written in Arabic script. The citizens of the empire, whether they were Turkish, Greek, Armenian, Arab, Albanian etc.

**PRIVY CHAMBER:** the sultan's private quarters, presumably where he ate and slept.

**SAFAVID:** from the name of the ancestral founder, Safi-al-din, of the ruling dynasty in Persia from circa 1500 to 1723.

**SARAY:** literally "palace".

**SHALVAR:** baggy drawstring pants tapered at the ankles worn by both men and women.

**SPOGLIA:** remains of earlier buildings used in later constructions.

**SULTAN:** the supreme head of the Ottoman Empire. Also, a title given to female relatives of the sultan, whether daughters, wives, or mothers.

**TOPKAPI:** Cannon Gate.

**TUĞRA:** the sultan's monogram, written in elaborate Arabic calligraphy, also attached to all official documents to confirm their legality.

**ULEMA:** the doctors of Islamic canon law, theology, and philosophy.

**UMAYYAD:** dynasty ruling from Damascus from 661 to 750, claiming to be descendants of the prophet Mohammed.

**VALIDE:** title given to the reigning sultan's mother, "Queen Mother".

**VIZIER:** minister of the Ottoman governing council.

# Illustration credits

* All other illustrations are original photographs by Murat Oğurlu.

# Bibliography

Bon, Ottavio. *Il Serraglio del Gransignore, a cura di Bruno Basile*. Rome: Salerno Editrice, 2002.

Çağman, Filiz. *Padişah Portreleri*. Istanbul: Yapı ve Kredi Bankası, 1984.

Davis, Fanny. *The Palace of Topkapi in Istanbul*. New York: Charles Scribner's Sons, 1970.

Eldem, Sedad and Akozan. *Topkapı Sarayı: Bir Mimari Araştırma*. İstanbul: Kültür ve Turizm Bakanlığı, 1982.

Ethem, Halil. *Topkapı Sarayı*. Istanbul: Kanaat Kütüphanesi, 1931.

Finkel, Caroline. *Osman's Dream; the Story of the Ottoman Empire*. London: John Murray Press, 2004 (forthcoming).

Imber, Colin. *The Ottoman Empire*. New York: Palgrave-Macmillan, 2002.

Inalcik, Halil. *The Ottoman Empire: The Classical Age 1300-1600*. London: Phoenix Press, 1997.

Ipşiroglu, M.S., *Bozkurt Ruzgârı Siyah Kalem*. Istanbul: Ada Yayınları, 1985.

Kocu, Resat Ekrem. "Topkapı Sarayı" in *Dünden Bugüne Istanbul Ansiklopedisi*. Istanbul: Kültür Bakanlığı ve Tarih Vakfı ve Türkiye Ekonomik ve Toplumsal Tarih Vakfı, 1993.

Lewis, Geoffrey, ed. *Domenico's Istanbul*. (M.J., L. Austin, translator) Warminster: Gibb Memorial Trust, 2001.

Mansel, Philip. *Constantinople, City of the World's Desire*. New York: St. Martin's Griffin, 1995.

Mantran, Robert, ed. *Histoire de l'Empire Ottoman*. Paris: Fayard, 1989.

Necipoglu, Gulru. *Architecture, Ceremonial and Power: The Topkapi Palace in the Fifteenth Century*. New York: M.I.T. Press, 1991.

Pedani, Maria Pia. "Safiye's Household and Venetian Diplomacy" in *TURCICA*. Vol. 32, 2000.

Peirce, Leslie P. *The Imperial Harem*. New York and Oxford: Oxford University Press, 1993.

Rogers, J.M., ed. *The Topkapi Saray Museum Vols. 1-5*. London and Boston: Thames and Hudson, 1986-1987.

Scott and Faik Yaltırık. *The Gardens of Turkey*. Istanbul: Türkiye Turing ve Otomobil Kurumu, 1989.

Tezcan, Hülya. *Topkapı Sarayı ve Çevresinin Bizans Devri Arkeolojisi*. Istanbul: Türkiye Turing ve Otomobil Kurumu, 1989.

*Palace of Gold and Light, Treasures of Topkapi Palace*. Istanbul: Palace Arts Foundation Catalogue to the Exhibition, Me-Pa, 2000.

*Rijksmuseum Amsterdam Highlights*. Amsterdam: Rijksmuseum-Stichting, 1995.

*The Art of Suleyman the Magnificent*. Sydney: International Cultural Corporation of Australia Ltd., 1990.

*Topkapi a Versailles*. Paris: Association Française d'Action Artistique, 1999.

"Yaratıcı Osmanlılar" in *Sanat Dunyamız*. Vol. 73, Yapı Kredi Yayınları, 1999.